RETREAT

TIME APART FOR
SILENCE & SOLITUDE

ROGER HOUSDEN

Thorsons

A LABYRINTH BOOK

RETREAT: TIME APART FOR SILENCE AND SOLITUDE

Thorsons
An imprint of HarperCollins*Publishers*
77–85 Fulham Palace Road,
Hammersmith, London W6 8JB

Published by Thorsons 1995
1 3 5 7 9 10 8 6 4 2

A catalogue record for this book is available from the British Library

ISBN 1 85538 490 6

Printed in ITALY by GRAPHICOM

Design by DW Design
Typesetting by DW Design in London, England

CONTENTS

RETREAT   1
SILENCE   4
MINDFULNESS   12
MEDITATION   17
THE RETREAT COMMUNITY   22
THE RETREAT LEADER   25

THE WAY OF KNOWLEDGE   29
BUDDHISM   29
ZEN BUDDHISM   37
TIBETAN BUDDHISM   48
RAJA YOGA   59
SHAMANISM   64

THE WAY OF THE HEART   79
CHRISTIANITY   79
SUFISM   102
BHAKTI YOGA   106

THE WAY OF THE BODY   115
TAI CHI   122
YOGA   127
PRAPTO MOVEMENT WORK - THE WALK OF LIFE   134

THE WAY OF ART   139
THE AWAKENED EYE   142
CAROLINE MACKENZIE   145

THE WAY OF SOUND   151
THE HEALING VOICE   158
THE NAKED VOICE   162

THE WAY OF THE WILDERNESS   167
JOURNEY INTO EMPTINESS   170
THE UPAYA FOUNDATION   174
THE TRACKING PROJECT   178

THE SOLITARY WAY   183
ASSAKREM   188
HALVET   192
THE THREE YEAR TIBETAN RETREAT   197

ADDRESSES   202
BIBLIOGRAPHY   210
INDEX   212
ACKNOWLEDGMENTS   216

RETREAT

TODAY, MORE PEOPLE ARE GOING ON RETREAT THAN EVER before. While the Christian monastic tradition is in decline all over the Western world, retreat facilities of every spiritual denomination are full weeks, even months, in advance. Though the noise and pace of contemporary life undoubtedly contributes to the current interest in retreats, there are other, more fundamental reasons for the rise in their popularity.

People who go on retreats today are not necessarily religious; they may come from any background and from any age range. What they have in common is a desire for silence, solitude and reflection. These desires are innate to the human condition: they are not bound to a particular time, religion or set of beliefs. For those who want spiritual guidance and training as well as simple solitude, there are many paths to choose from.

The concept of retreat has always been connected to a spiritual discipline and was often taken to extraordinary lengths: a film called *Anchorite*, which appeared in 1994, tells the story of a fourteenth century Irish woman who chose to be walled up in a cell for her entire life. Traditionally, the retreat has been seen within a monastic context and the purpose has always been to find God, or to attain a deep insight into existence and one's own individual nature.

Spiritual retreats are more popular than ever, although they rarely entail the intensity and privations of medieval fervor (exceptions are certain Tibetan and Sufi retreats, described in the Solitary Retreats section). The division between secular and sacred is less sharp now; attitudes to the body and the sensual life have softened and the retreat is no longer seen as an escape from an evil world. Now that every spiritual tradition can be found in any major western city, extremist

Right: The popular concept of retreat has traditionally been connected to spiritual discipline, and centered around silence, solitude and prayer.

Previous pages: Space and silence offers the natural setting in which to reflect.

Opposite: Retreats today take many different forms: intense physical activity can lead to deep insight and focus.

and absolutist views are giving way to broader, more relative perspectives. The retreat is seen as a temporary withdrawal designed to empower the individual to fulfill his or her spiritual value within the context of everyday life.

A contemporary retreat may consist of anything from an arduous spiritual discipline to an art class or a hike through wild and sacred terrain. Which ever you choose, the broad common purpose remains the same: to return the individual to themselves through the cultivation of silence and awareness. This book is written for every one of us in whom the need for silence and reflection is present. Different kinds of retreats are categorized according to the temperaments they broadly respond to; thus retreats described under *The Way of Knowledge* include Buddhist, Raja Yoga and Shamanistic retreats as, while these traditions vary greatly from each other in many respects, they all act on the nature of the mind and seek the awakening of knowledge within the practitioner. Retreats in these traditions will tend to take place with this in view, although it will be expressed differently in each of them.

Christian, Sufi and Bhakti Yoga retreats are described in the section, *The Way of the Heart.* These traditions can all be characterized by an emphasis on the transformation of the feeling, rather than the thinking, of the practitioner. Other ways described in the book have no specific religious background at all. A wilderness retreat simply

requires a love of nature and a wish to be immersed in it: nature can be the source of a person's deepest insights and inspirations. So can art or singing, other popular ways of retreat. Finally *The Solitary Way* can encompass any or all of the other ways. You may spend time alone on a mountain or in a desert, without any specific aim other than to experience solitude. You may go on a Native American "Vision Quest," take a solitary spiritual retreat as prescribed by the Sufis, or even the three year Tibetan Retreat.

It is important to remember that the different categories are meant to serve as general indications only, not as solid dividing lines. Many Buddhist practices generate feelings of devotion and compassion, while an extensive body of knowledge underpins all Sufi devotional music, dance and chanting. The background to the traditions is given, so that the reader may better understand the broader context in which a particular retreat takes place. Which ever way you choose, the retreat will be largely determined by your own motivation and intention. You will get out of it what you put in: in fact, you will even get more, because the retreat will magnify your intention, not only through the discipline of spiritual practices but by the nature of the retreat context itself. If the five factors of the retreat (silence, mindfulness, meditation, the retreat community and the retreat leader) are fully appreciated, the retreat is bound to bring its rewards.

*The contemplative waits in silence
and when he is 'answered',
it is not so much by a word
that bursts into his silence.
It is by this silence itself suddenly,
inexplicably, revealing itself to him
as a word of great power.*

Thomas Merton,
Contemplative Prayer.

SILENCE

THERE IS A MAN IN INDIA CALLED CHANDRA Swami who, more than twenty years ago, chose not to speak. He has not uttered a word since. He is one of the most vital, radiant people you could meet and, when asked why he still keeps his vow after all this time, writes simply that he has fallen in love with the silence. He no longer needs it as a discipline but can see no reason to abandon a source of continuing joy.

Twenty years may seem a little extreme but the Swami is far from alone: to devote an extended period, even a whole lifetime, to silence, is a common practice among religious people of all

traditions. The Swami's feeling of being in love with silence is shared by renunciates the world over. The rule of silence is integral to the Carthusian Order of catholic monks and is usual for some period of the day in religious orders of all denominations. A retreat for lay people, whether for a weekend or a year, is usually held all or partly in silence. Silence is one of the boundaries that sets a retreat apart from the affairs of daily living.

The reasons for this are simple. A period of silence allows us to be less involved in the social self, creating room for both the world beyond

our immediate concerns and for the deeper reaches of our own being.

Silence proclaims the beauty and grandeur of life more eloquently than the tongue. We are normally too busy listening to our unceasing interior monologue to give undivided attention to what lies around us. There is a well-known meditation exercise that leads us into silence by encouraging us to listen more deeply to our surroundings. We start by sitting quietly in an erect and comfortable position, listening to our own breathing. We enlarge our listening to encompass the room we are sitting in. Slowly we listen for sound coming from elsewhere in the house. Then we include the sounds outside, the birds, the lawnmower, the traffic. By extending the range of our listening in this way the mind can become less obsessed with particular concerns and more sensitive to the space in which all sounds are happening.

Spiritual traditions of every kind perceive that space, or spaciousness, to be the fundamental nature of the mind itself. It is always there, in the gap between thoughts and beneath our words and, when we give time

Right: *Religious disciplines throughout the world recognize the importance of observing outer silence.*

Previous pages:
4. *Chandra Swami, who expresses joy through silence and prayer.*

5. *Spaciousness is perceived to be the fundamental nature of the mind itself.*

to listening for that silence, it is naturally more likely to reveal itself. This is why observing outer silence is an important aspect of a retreat: it helps us to enter the inner silence of our deeper nature.

Vivekenanda, the sage who first brought the wisdom of India to the West at the turn of the century, said that silence was the loudest form of prayer. Ramana Maharshi, one of the greatest teachers that India has ever produced, said,

"Silence, which is devoid of the

Left: *"Silence like the sunlight will illuminate you in God..."*

assertive ego, alone is liberation." He was referring to a merging with the silence that lies at the heart of every human being. Ramana considered silence to be the most direct teaching he could give his disciples. In this he was following an ancient tradition in India; the quasi-mythical teacher, Dakshinamurti, is reputed to have brought four learned sages to self-realization through the power of his silence. When Ramana was asked why he did not go about and teach the people at large, he replied,

"What do you think of a man who listens to a sermon for an hour and goes away without having been impressed by it so as to change his life? Compare him with another, who sits in a holy presence and goes away after some time with his outlook on life totally changed. Which is the better, to preach loudly without effect or to sit silently sending out inner force?"

(David Goodman, *Be As You Are*.)

One of the early desert fathers, the Syrian monk, Isaac of Ninevah, says the same thing in Christian terms:

"Every man who delights in a multitude of words, even though he says admirable things, is empty within. If you love truth, be a lover of silence. Silence like the sunlight will illuminate you in God and will deliver you from the phantoms of ignorance. Silence will unite you to God himself...

More than all things love silence: it brings you a fruit that tongue cannot describe. In the beginning we have to force ourselves to be silent. But then there is born something that draws us to silence. May God give you an experience of this "something" that is born of silence. If only you practice this, untold light will dawn on you in consequence... after a while a certain sweetness is born in the heart of this exercise and the body is drawn almost by force to remain in silence."

(Thomas Merton, *Contemplative Prayer*.)

Below: *An ancient portrait of Bodhidharma, the founder of Chinese Zen Buddhism.*

Opposite: *India must be one of the noisiest places on earth: the contemporary world is fraught with daily babble.*

Bodhidharma, who made a pilgrimage in the late fifth century from his native India to China, was the founder of Chinese Zen Buddhism. Impoverished, emaciated and in tatters after years of begging and wandering, he was received by Emperor Wu in his throne room. The Emperor asked: "What is the deepest meaning of the holy truth?" Bodhidharma's answer consisted of just four words: "Open spaces, nothing holy." When the mind is spacious, it has room for everything. There is no longer any distinction between sacred and secular.

Silence works not only on the inmost reaches of the soul but at the more tangible and mundane level of the body. It is a physical relief to be silent, in a silent environment, even for a day. Noise pollution is one of the principal causes of stress in the western world. It is the single largest factor in neighbor disputes in Britain. Over one third of all complaints received by the police and the local councils are associated with noisy neighbors.

The "mystical East" is not immune: India must be one of the noisiest places on earth. There is a temple in every village; every temple now has a loudspeaker, which blares out devotional songs in modern, film music idiom, from 3.00AM to 6.00AM in the morning. Ninety per cent of the traffic on any Indian road is commercial and every lorry driver's fist is continually pressed on a type of horn which makes Italian traffic sound positively genteel.

In the West, it seems we are almost afraid of silence. We seem desperate to fill every corner and every occasion with muzak, drum machines and synthesized, stupefying rhythms. Lifts, shopping malls, hotel lobbies, airports, almost every public space is plastered with a thick coating of musical mediocrity. Even without the muzak, the contemporary world is fraught with a daily babble. In her novel, *Oranges Are Not The Only Fruit*, Jeannette Winterson comes up with an inventive, if partial solution. She has a sky cleaner come on duty every night and mop up all the verbal flotsam and jetsam floating over the city. We would do better to address the cause. Imagine what Paris or New York would be like if, for even ten minutes a day, everyone went about their business without speaking.

It won't happen, which is why retreat centers everywhere are full months in advance. Doing nothing other than sitting and listening, the

Opposite: *People from all nationalities have, throughout history, chosen to retreat from everyday noise and bustle to live in quietude and devotion.*

Right: *A time of silence and contemplation can focus thought and attention, altering one's perception of the world.*

world starts to come alive again; and more, we come alive to ourselves. There is a lot to be said for not speaking. We might feel sympathy for Wordsworth who, in the first of four sonnets he wrote called *Personal Talk*, said:

> *"I am not one who oft much or oft delight*
> *To season my fireside with personal talk...*
> *Better than such discourse doth silence long...*
> *To sit without emotion, hope, or aim,*
> *In the loved presence of my cottage fire*
> *And listen to the flapping of the flame*
> *Or kettle whispering its faint undersong..."*

After even a few hours of silence, we are more gathered, more contained, more present to ourselves than if we had flung words over our friends like confetti. We begin to sense the weight of words, how potent they can be and how wise it is not to waste them. Our own speaking, after an interim of silence, carries our true meaning more easily. It has a tone, a stillness, that will make others happy to listen and reminds us all that what we say matters.

*There are occasions
when you can hear the
mysterious language of the Earth,
in water, or coming through the trees,
emanating from the mosses, seeping through
the undercurrents of the soil;
but you have to be willing
to wait and receive.*

John Hay
The Immortal Wilderness

MINDFULNESS

MINDFULNESS, ATTENTION, AWARENESS, REMEMBERING, presence—every tradition has a different name for this quality of being. At any moment, its measure is the measure of what a person is and what a group of people are.

Most of the time our attention is dispersed between a variety of different preoccupations: it is actually quite rare that we give ourselves to just one thing at a time. Eating breakfast, we may be talking to our family, opening the mail, listening to the radio, reading the paper and wondering whether we should phone that important client now or later. Consequently, none of these activities receives our full attention. We spend much of our lives not being present in the moment we are living.

Focusing attention in one place, being present to the moment at hand, is one of the most enlivening, enriching things we can do. Ordinarily, attention comes and goes without our consent. Rather than being something we do, it is something that happens to us, as things and thoughts grab our attention. When the stimulus goes, so does the attention it commanded; we sink back into our habitual state of dispersion until the next attention-getter comes along. Active attention is different. It is generated consciously from inside us by a decision—an intention to be aware of where we are. To make that decision takes no more than a split second. It is easy, involving no more than a shift of the attention away from the periphery to the center. What is not easy is to enforce that decision again and again,

from moment to moment. The decision is not a result of discursive reasoning, or a sheer act of will; it derives from the insight that one is less alive than one would like and that this condition arises from our dispersion. Acknowledging the truth of our condition is already an act of gathering ourselves together. We have brought our attention to ourselves; not to the flow of our thoughts and feelings but to the sensation of ourselves, to our own presence, or lack of it.

When, through a moment of seeing what is happening to us, we free ourselves from the grip of self-preoccupation, our natural presence arises. The energy that was locked up in our concerns is free to manifest as the delight of open and spacious awareness. The Zen Buddhists call it the "beginner's mind."

In every moment of absorbed attention we are open to the unexpected. "Attention, attention, attention," wrote Zen Master Ikkyu centuries ago when asked what was the highest wisdom. This is the heart of Zen practice. Zen monks have for centuries used traditional arts as a vehicle for active attention as today, an arts or a Zen retreat, will emphasize the same thing. One can only write authentically if one is so joined to the words one is writing. Then, one is no longer writing "about" something: one's experience is the word on the page. There is no gap in that moment between writer and word.

This presence is also encouraged in the wilderness retreat. Nature can often shock the mind away from its habitual preoccupations by the sheer impact of its beauty, grandeur and power. Nature invites us

Left: *The miracle of the world around us is an endless source of spiritual nourishment for those who are truly aware.*

Previous page: *Absorbed, mindful awareness opens the mind to incredible spaciousness.*

to listen and join it in its teeming aliveness. John Hay, in *Parabola Magazine*, has written: "There are occasions when you can hear the mysterious language of the Earth, in water, or coming through the trees, emanating from the mosses, seeping through the undercurrents of the soil; but you have to be willing to wait and receive."

Thich Nhat Hanh is a Zen Master from Vietnam who now lives in France. In his book *The Miracle of Mindfulness*, he writes: "I think the real miracle is not to walk either on water or in thin air but to walk on earth. Every day we are engaged in a miracle which we don't even recognize: a blue sky, white clouds, green leaves, the black, curious eyes of a child–our own two eyes. All is a miracle." To know that miracle is to be present to oneself and to the world. Tai, as he is known to his students, emphasizes how important this presence is in the most mundane of activities. "When you are washing dishes, washing dishes must be the most important thing in your life. When you're using the toilet, let that be the most important thing in your life." We can use the very activities that usually distract us as reminders to wake up. He suggests that, before answering the telephone, we let it ring three times and return to ourselves by becoming aware of our breathing. Or when we are about to start the car, we wait and bring our awareness to three breaths before turning the key.

Awareness of the breath is a common technique for returning to the present moment in all spiritual traditions. So is the repetition of God's name or names and the use of the rosary. The Sufis, the mystics of Islam, use bodily movements and intensifying the attention on a chosen part of the body for a specified period during daily life. They

Right: *Disciplines such as calligraphy have been used for centuries as a path towards greater enlightenment.*

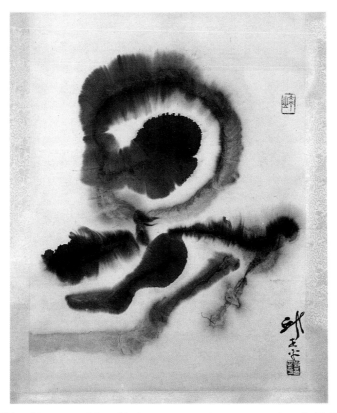

might allot fifteen minutes a day to developing the sensation in the left hand. While a Zen Buddhist might turn any daily activity into an end in itself as a practice of awareness, a Theravadin Buddhist might practice being aware of the stream of his thoughts. Whatever the method, the intent is the same.

Christianity places emphasis on recollection. Keeping one's mind on God and doing all for His glory can be seen as a means of bringing the mind round to one place. The greatest manual of spiritual training in the Christian world is undoubtedly *The Philokalia*, the collection of early writings at the center of Orthodox monasticism. The need for attentiveness is called for throughout. In it, Saint Simeon the New Theologian says,

"In a word, he who does not have attention in himself and does not guard his mind, cannot become pure in heart and cannot see God....

Speaking generally, it is impossible to acquire virtue in any other way except through this kind of attention. Therefore you should try to gain this more than anything else, so as to learn what I tell you in your own experience... Keep your attention within yourself (not in your head but in your heart). Keep your mind there (in your heart), trying by every possible means to find the place where the heart is, in order that, having found it, your mind should constantly abide there. Wrestling thus, the mind will find the place of the heart." (*Writings from the Philokalia.*)

To go on retreat is to have already taken the decision to set time apart from everyday distractions; to gather the attention for a period of time. The very context and atmosphere of a retreat is designed so that "the mind can find the place in the heart." This is the essence of mindfulness.

> *If you seek Him*
> *you shall never find Him.*
> *If you do not seek Him,*
> *He will never reveal*
> *Himself to you.*
>
> **Old Sufi saying**

MEDITATION

SOME OF THE MANY APPROACHES TO MEDITATION WILL BE discussed more specifically in the following sections of this book, since most retreats, though not all, involve meditation of some kind. The aim here is to offer a broad understanding of what meditation is and to point to some of the attitudes and perspectives that are common to meditation in all traditions.

Meditation is sometimes described as our natural state. No tradition or technique can claim it for its own. I did not come to meditation as a Buddhist, a Christian, or anything in particular; as a university student, I used to find myself sitting quietly, eyes open, falling into a state of silent communion with the natural environment. The experience was not something extraordinary or special, simply the delight of just being there. Far from being a withdrawal from the world, the activity was one of entering more fully and deeply into it, so that I and my environment were part of the same unity. I was not aware that I was meditating as such; I just knew it as a simple facility for slipping into the spaciousness behind thoughts.

I only discovered much later that this was what people called meditation. Meditation, then, is a progressively deeper recognition of what is already here. It is not so much an attempt to penetrate the mystery, more an active willingness to be open, receptive and attentive, so that Whatever Is might reveal Itself. In the most profound sense, meditation leads to the falling away of our ordinary, habitual self and the recognition of our true identity.

There are a bewildering number of meditation techniques which aim to effect this in different ways. Which specific path we choose or bump into is usually a matter of individual disposition. Buddhists may say they are practicing meditation in order to arrive at enlightenment;

Right: Meditation is sometimes described as our natural state: but we should not allow the bewildering array of techniques to distract us from the aim.

Previous page: Meditation can take many forms and is an intensely personal discipline.

Christians, that they are surrendering to God; Sufis or Hindus might want to sail out of the body altogether on the wings of absorption and return full of bliss and the ineffable. Common to them all are certain attitudes that are inherent to the nature of meditation itself and perhaps, even, indispensable to it.

One of these attitudes is the willingness to acknowledge that we do not know who we are, what we are sitting down to, even what the real point of meditation is. In our daily activities, we usually seem quite clear about what we are doing, who we are and where we are going. Life is generally under control and we seem to call the tune. In meditation, our certainty soon disappears. We do not have to sit for long before becoming uncomfortably aware of our dispersion and of the way our attention leaps out of control at the most insignificant passing thought. We soon start to sense that we are less solid than we imagined.

Often the act of meditation is no more than the willingness to sit in the midst of the awareness of our lack of any real motivation and of any particular feeling other than, perhaps, boredom or frustration. Just sitting with this, not trying to change it, do anything about it or judge it can open a broader view. Even the broader view, though, may have no consolations. This simple sitting can be arduous; it is sitting for no reason. With nowhere to go, the sense of absence has to be sufficient in itself. Meditation is often not interesting; it is not a diversion, it is the willingness to be with what is. Often, especially to begin with,

"what is" is the painful revelation of our fragmented self. Yet for Thomas Merton, this was the gateway to the deepest prayer of all, the prayer of the desert:

"Contemplative prayer is, in a way, simply the preference for the desert, for emptiness, for poverty... Only when we are able to "let go" of everything within us, all desire to see, to know, to taste and to experience the presence of God, do we truly become able to experience that presence with the overwhelming conviction and reality that revolutionizes our entire inner life." (*Contemplative Prayer*.)

When we start each meditation as if it were the first one, without any preconceived notion of what may or may not happen, whatever we experience is not judged as good or bad but is simply seen as phenomena unfolding on the screen of the mind. In sitting down to meditate, we do not know what we are sitting down to. Certainly there are steps to be taken that quieten the body and mind and that can help to bring us more into the moment. There can come a point when technique falls away and leaves us in–or as–a Vastness, a vibrant and spacious stillness that no words can articulate. For the anonymous author of *The Cloud of Unknowing*, that Vastness was complete darkness, a transparent nothingness which thickened the more he entered into it. He speaks of an apprehension, a trembling of the mind if not the body, at the intimation of its possible undoing. When we reach those depths, we are truly set before the Unknown, exposing the deepest layers of humanity and of life itself.

Another theme common to all forms of meditation is the paradox of needing to make an effort on the one hand and to be receptive and open on the other. There is an old Sufi saying which points to the razor's edge that we need to follow between effort and no effort:

If you seek Him you shall never find Him.
If you do not seek Him,
He will never reveal Himself to you.

Our intention is normally tied to a method, be it following the breath, repeating a name or resting one's eyes on a white wall. While keeping our attention on the method, without straining or forcing ourselves, we are also called to remain in a posture of openness and availability to ourselves and whatever arises; to the thoughts and feelings that we would rather not hear. Being available means not interfering, not trying to change or control what happens; simply staying attentive, awake to life as it unfolds.

There is a deeper availability still, which brings us to the theme of surrender. We may begin the meditation with nothing more than a sense of dispersion and scattered will; we may be fired with a burning intention; or we may have a quiet wish to enter the silence. Whatever our hope, meditation will take us to the point when we need to surrender it to whatever lies beyond our experience. Meditation will always point further than where we are.

Like everything else we do, meditation is usually anchored in the body. Though there are some spiritual traditions—notably the Sufis and some branches of Raja Yoga—that use meditation as a means of leaving

Left: *Every-day activities such as reading, walking or even gardening can all become powerful forms of meditation.*

Right: *An additional focus, such as these prayer beads, can often help bring the mind closer to awareness.*

bodily consciousness behind, most traditions make use of the body, or an aspect of its functioning, like breathing, to anchor the awareness in the present moment. The body, after all, is always present here and now; it is we who are usually absent. Returning to the body is to return to ourselves and reality. As our meditation deepens, that reality becomes less concrete than it usually appears to be. The body becomes lighter, more alive with energy; instead of being perceived as separate from other objects and separate from the mind, it becomes part of the flow of life so that the body, the mind and the world itself are felt to be aspects of one life that is living us. This experience of non-separateness is central to every form of meditation, in every tradition.

Though this section has been titled *Meditation,* I have used the word only because of its current coinage. Its Latin roots and its adoption by the Christian orthodoxy to mean reflection, pondering a subject, give it a slant that allows for none of the subtleties of the Buddhist and Hindu practices that are all lumped under the one English term. There are other, more archaic, words which may be more appropriate and accurate for the deeper stages of what we have been describing: contemplation, for example, and prayer. What meditation ultimately points to is a wordless prayer of the whole being; not a plea to some vague entity but a silent gesture of receptivity to the mystery and immensity of life

In all the three worlds there is no boat like Satsanga to carry one safely across the ocean of births and deaths.

Be As You Are
David Godman

THE RETREAT COMMUNITY

MANY PEOPLE MEDITATE ALONE TODAY WITHOUT THE guidance of a teacher or the support of a community. People sing, dance or write on their own without ever showing their work to anyone else. Personal experience is often given more credence than external authority. This is hardly surprising, since the traditional authority of family, church and state has long been in steep decline and absolute authority of any kind is hard to justify but how can we know the value of our own work, the reality of our own meditative experience, without any reference to an external sounding board? As Philip Novak writes in *Parabola,* "A New Age movement that wishes to champion contemplative technique but jettison the traditional context

in which it was originally lodged seems likely to be either very superficial or very dangerous or both." Although Christianity, in particular, has often served to repress rather than acknowledge individual insight and vision, it–like every other tradition–has also acted as an objective body of knowledge and authority against which the individual might assess the authenticity of his or her own inner voice. This was, and still remains, the great value of working within the context of a spiritual tradition.

The Western spiritual heritage has always mistrusted, even feared, the authority of subjective experience. In monastic communities, mystical experience was not encouraged or favored; daily work and

the communal liturgy were the rules of the day and the ecstatic songs and visions of a John of the Cross or a Teresa of Avila were the exception, not the rule. As a result, Christianity now finds itself sadly lacking in methods and practices of contemplation and without the formidable and sophisticated maps of Eastern traditions, whose foundations rest on empirical observation and practice. Having for centuries relied so heavily on external authority, the spiritual heritage of the West is now ill-equipped to serve us in this age, which places such emphasis on the value of subjective experience.

Eastern disciplines have rushed in to fill the breach. Buddhism, especially, makes available teachings and methods that provide an objective mirror for personal insight, as well as the means to cultivate it. However, like any other tradition today, it does not and cannot have the voice of absolute authority. The era of absolute truth is over. The aberrations and idiosyncrasies of all traditions become plain when they rub shoulders as intimately as they do today. In the contemporary world, the spiritual community, in all its many forms, offers a bridge between external and inner authority. Our own peers can reflect to us the validity of our personal understanding and hearing the experiences of others can put our own into perspective. Spiritual communities are regrouping themselves in many forms which include, but are not limited to, the contexts of traditional disciplines. The

Right: *Prayer at the Kagyu Center.*

Left: *Master Sheng-Yen,*
Zen master and teacher.

Previous page: *Retreatants make*
offerings at the Kagyu Center in the
Dordogne, France.

retreat is a temporary spiritual community that agrees to come together for a specific length of time for a specific purpose. One need not be a Buddhist to attend a Buddhist retreat; the allegiance is not necessarily to the umbrella tradition but rather to the retreat itself and its task in hand.

As well as providing for feedback, the retreat community offers a context for people of like mind to put their will in one direction. The intention of an individual is always strengthened when surrounded by people with the same aspiration. Writing, meditating or singing can be lonely occupations and the encouragement of allies is always an invaluable support.

The power of collective agreement exists in a retreat to empower the individual's intention. A body of rules is accepted by the community; a timetable, perhaps and the particular method or practice to be adopted. There are commonly rules that exclude sexual contact, smoking and cosmetics, regulate the intake of food and exclude meat

and stimulants. The rules are the results of the culled experience of generations of retreatants and monastics before us and are freely accepted by the individual for the duration of the retreat.

Three days or so into retreat, the individual will often become aware of a collective presence, the combined humanity of the group. He will come to notice how everyone has their own idiosyncrasies; his own particular tendencies will become as obvious as those of others. From this realization, tolerance will often arise; even a sense of love for the others and their essential humanity. The natural sharing of loving kindness, in silence, is one of the richest gifts a retreat community can offer and it is part of what is meant by *satsang*, the Hindu term for a spiritual gathering. *Satsang* means nothing less than "association with truth, or reality," and Sankara, the great eighth century teacher of Advaita Vedanta, said, "In all the three worlds there is no boat like Satsanga to carry one safely across the ocean of births and deaths." (David Goodman, *Be As You Are.*)

*If you disregard Shih-fu
(the master), it is like a pilot disregarding
the directions of the control tower. If he
disobeys, disaster will happen. So Shih-fu is
like a compass, or a control tower ...*

Master Sheng-yen.
Getting the Buddha Mind,

THE
RETREAT
LEADER

THE LEADER OF A RETREAT MAY BE SOMEONE WHO HAS developed a skill or technique to a point where she or he is able to impart it to others, or a sage who is the embodiment of the highest spiritual teachings. Between the two lies a vast range of abilities and degrees of personal and spiritual integration.

At one end of the spectrum of spiritual teachers is the guru. No word provokes reaction faster among spiritual aspirants than this simple Hindu term.

It conjures an image of absolute, even tyrannical, authority. It suggests—to the Western mind, at least—the abnegation of personal responsibility and discernment. The whole matter of surrender—without even entering into the question of surrender of what and to whom, which will be addressed in later sections of this book—is a difficult one for the Western personality, whose basis is normally the quest for identity and individuality. Although the relationship between guru and disciple is a time-tested, time-honored tradition, gurus do not have an untarnished name in the West and the practitioner should be as awake as possible to the authority he may be placing himself under.

The Buddhist traditions place strong emphasis on the teacher-practitioner relationship, especially Tibetan Buddhism. In a retreat which is open to the general public, rather than exclusively to disciples, the Tibetans conduct themselves in the same way as their counterparts in Vipassana and Zen; they will expect their authority to be fully acknowledged but to end with the retreat. During a Buddhist retreat, the teacher can be expected to offer support to the effort of the retreatants, the teaching itself and his own authority as an embodiment of the teaching. In a Zen retreat, the teacher represents his lineage. What he transmits through that lineage is the Buddha-mind itself: the practitioner can "catch" the Buddha-mind through the intensity of his own faith and practice and the fundamental role of the Zen master is to confirm the practitioner's experience. Master Sheng-Yen, who runs Ch'an (Chinese Zen) retreats in New York, the United Kingdom and Taiwan, writes this on the place of the teacher:

"If you disregard Shih-fu (the master), it is like a pilot disregarding the directions of the control tower. If he disobeys, disaster will happen. So Shih-fu is like a compass, or a control tower. Time and

Left: *The Dalai Lama surrounded by disciples.*

Below: *Sathya Sai Baba makes an offering.*

again he corrects and adjusts your practice, leading you forward. You should understand that this faith in Shih-fu is really faith in the Buddha Dharma which Shih-fu represents. You must believe in him one hundred per cent. Forget your past and future. Don't cling to any viewpoints." (Master Sheng-yen, *Getting the Buddha Mind.*)

Many of the misunderstandings about the relationship between master and student occur because such a relationship has been imported from the East into a Western context that simply has no references of its own by which to judge it. The Dalai Lama, when asked about unscrupulous teachers, says that Westerners try to surrender too quickly. He points out that in the Tibetan tradition "a student spends years with a teacher observing his behavior, questioning others about him, noting whether he lives the principles he teaches, before deciding to take him on as a guru. Indeed, in the early years of practice, students are encouraged to doubt both teachers and

teachings." This was taken from an article written by Stephen Bodian in his book, *Living Yoga*. Bodian goes on to offer some simple but excellent suggestions for someone who is looking for a teacher:

1. *Trust your common sense and intuition: there is a deeper place, in the gut, where you know what is going on.*
2. *Feel free to question and doubt.*
3. *Keep your wits about you—beware of hidden persuasions and other attempts to take advantage of others by bypassing the rational mind in the name of some higher value, like love or devotion.*
4. *Maintain firm boundaries—don't relinquish your right to say no.*
5. *The true guru is inside you—the ultimate authority is nowhere but in our own hearts. Mother Meera says, "If any human guru is giving you teachings that bring you closer in your heart to the Divine, listen and be grateful and follow them. But be clear about the limitations of all human gurus."*

THE WAY OF KNOWLEDGE

BUDDHISM

I N THE LAST TWENTY YEARS NO SPIRITUAL TRADITION IN THE Western world has gained so many adherents as Buddhism. In 1980 there were just four Buddhist centers in the United Kingdom. Now there are almost two hundred, with many more in the USA. While the monastic population of Christianity is decreasing year on year, new Buddhist monasteries are springing up in every country in Europe and all over the USA.

Buddhism clearly responds to needs that traditional religion does not supply. One reason for its success is its avoidance of dogma and its insistence on the need of people to verify the truth of the teachings for themselves. Buddhism is inherently practical. It is a way of knowledge that is gained by first-hand experience. The Buddha said, in one of his sermons:

"Come, Kalamas, do not be satisfied with hearsay or with tradition... When you know in yourselves "These ideas are unprofitable" then you should abandon them. When you know in yourselves, "These things are profitable," then you should practice and abide in them." (Nanamoli Kandy, *The Life of the Buddha*.)

Buddhism has a long tradition of free inquiry and consequently a respect for others who find truth in their different ways. On the whole, Buddhism has kept itself remarkably free of inquisitions, religious wars and the like. It is not centered around a body of beliefs that have to be

Below: *A sesshin, or intensive
training period, at a Zen
Buddhist retreat.*

Previous pages:
*28. A disciple of the Dalai Lama
celebrating the Kalachakra
festival in Sarnath, India.*

*29. The door to the entrance hall
of the Rumtek Monastery.*

defended; rather, Buddhism offers things to do: a wide array of spiritual practices as well as moral precepts, to help the practitioner to penetrate the mystery of life and see the truth with his own eyes. Instead of addressing metaphysical questions like "What happens to us after death?" or "Who made the world?" Buddhism encourages us to inquire into the nature of life as we experience it and to verify for ourselves the Four Noble Truths that the Buddha taught in his first sermon in the Deer Park at Isipatana, in India:

1. *Suffering exists*
2. *All suffering has a cause*
3. *That cause may be terminated*
4. *The means of termination is
   the following of the Noble
   Eightfold Path*

To realize the first truth, we need to see life with a realistic–not pessimistic–outlook, which is usually the result of considerable life experience. We need to have seen how often we are not content with where we are or who we are and how often we forsake our present reality for dreams of the future or memories of the past. This leads us to the second Noble Truth, that the cause of our suffering is our dissatisfaction with life as it is and our desire to reach out for something else. The third truth tells us there is a way out of this eternal round of dissatisfaction and longing. There is a dimension of existence that lies beyond birth

and death, which can be known here and now. The Buddhist term for this is Nirvana, the pristine mind that always exists beneath our flow of thoughts and feelings. The way to experience the clear mind of Nirvana is to practice the Noble Eightfold Path:

1. Right Understanding
2. Right Thought
3. Right Speech
4. Right Action
5. Right Livelihood
6. Right Effort
7. Right Mindfulness
8. Right Concentration

The Eightfold Path, then, consists in the cultivation of wisdom, morality and meditation. Right understanding is gained by hearing and absorbing the wisdom of the Buddha's teachings, while right thought concerns our motivation. Buddhist morality is similar to that of every spiritual tradition, though right action includes refraining from taking life of any kind. Right livelihood is based on the virtue of causing no harm to others, including the environment. The last two sections of the eightfold path concern meditation, the way by which the causes of our suffering may be seen clearly and ended. For lay people, the most appropriate way to learn and practice meditation is on a retreat. The various Buddhist schools lay emphasis on different methods.

THE THERAVADA SCHOOL

THE THERAVADA SCHOOL OF BUDDHISM ORIGINATED IN SRI Lanka and extends today throughout South Asia. It is traditionally more oriented towards renunciates than many other Buddhist schools and tends towards a transcendent rather than immanent view of the world. It is primarily represented in the West by people who have studied in Thailand, especially in the Forest Tradition that flourishes in the north-east of that country. The teacher there who has exerted the strongest influence on westerners is Ajahn Cha, who has trained many western monks at Wat Nong Pah Pong in Ubon Province. His foremost Western disciple is the American-born Ajahn Sumedho Thera, who founded the Chithurst Forest Monastery in rural southern England. Amaravati, a larger center near London, has been running for some years and branches exist in various parts of the world.

The other strong Theravadin influence in the West has come from Burma, in particular from the intensive meditation practices developed by masters like Mahasi Sayadaw and U Ba Khin. Ba Khin's method involves sweeping the body with attention and becoming aware of the play of sensations. His method has been spread around the world by the well-known teacher, S. N. Goenka.

Theravada meditation practice consists of samatha (tranquillity), sattipathana (mindful awareness) and vipassana (mindful awareness). In samatha, you give your attention to a single object, usually the breath or the sensations in the body. The traditional texts suggest various choices of object but the guiding rule is that they should be unexciting and neutral. What ever you use, no attempt should be made to alter it. If you use the breath you simply watch it, as it comes through the nostrils or rises and falls in the abdomen. Whenever you notice your attention wandering, you bring it back to the breath. Gradually, the mind will quieten and the practitioner will be established enough to move on to sattipathana. Attention is directed

Opposite: *The folded hands of a Buddhist monk reveal centeredness and peace.*

Left: *Buddhist monks in London.*

in a systematic way to what are known as the four foundations of mindfulness:

1. Bodily activity
2. Feelings
3. States of mind
4. Mental contents

The practitioner is developing a "witness" consciousness that allows him to see whatever phenomena enters the mind without reacting to it.

The aim of the third stage, vipassana, is to see through phenomenal existence altogether. The mind is opened to include anything that comes into its orbit. Often Theravada retreats are inaccurately referred to in the West as vipassana, whereas they often consist of the first two stages rather than the third one, vipassana itself.

What ever arises, whether it is submerged psychological material, in the form of old fears and past traumas, or states of bliss and peace, the purpose of vipassana is the same: to look with bare attention through all that comes to the mind and to see that whatever it is, it passes away. The practitioner neither rejects nor accepts the passing phenomena but sees through it with a neutral eye. In seeing that everything which comes to mind also goes, he has the insight that there is no central self made up of solid thoughts and feelings, only clear spaciousness, nirvana. That is the true nature of everything, including the meditator himself. To see this and to abide as this is the ultimate aim of Buddhist meditation in all its forms.

A complementary form of meditation which is usually practiced in conjunction with the three stages described above is called metta, the practice of loving kindness. This is common to all forms of Buddhism and probably stems from the realization on the part of the practicing Buddhist community that loving kindness and the qualities of equanimity, compassion and joy are the natural by-products of a spacious mind. A retreat in the Theravada tradition will often include a period of metta meditation, which involves generating the feeling of loving kindness towards oneself and others.

Left: *Meditating at
the Insight
Meditation Center,
Barre, Massachusetts.*

Below: *The Insight
Meditation Center.*

THE INSIGHT MEDITATION SOCIETY

"God, did I get bored. Sitting, walking, sitting, walking, lunch. Sitting, walking, sitting, walking, dinner. Five days without all my usual hits: no talking, no smoking, no cappuccino, no deals, no important phone calls. Yet by the time I got to the end, I didn't want to leave. What my time at IMS did was to show me—in between the bouts of boredom and irritation—that there was more to life, and more to myself, than just the next deal: that I could actually feel more alive than I had ever felt, just by sitting doing nothing, watching my thoughts go by. I had never given myself permission to do that before."

J. M., New York.

IMS, THE LARGEST OF THE AMERICAN VIPASSANA CENTERS, WAS founded in 1975 to offer vipassana retreats to both beginning and experienced meditators. Retreats vary in length from a weekend to three months and are led by one or more of the twenty teachers who are either living at IMS, or work there on a regular basis. A typical daily schedule begins at 5.00AM and ends at 10.00PM. Every day will be spent in silent practice with alternate periods of sitting and walking meditation. Daily instruction in meditation and nightly Dharma talks are given. Individuals have interviews with the teacher at regular intervals. In honor of the Buddhist tradition of dana (generosity), the teachers do not receive payment for leading retreats and course registration fees only cover the operating costs of the center. Meals are vegetarian and the accommodation is very simple, mostly in double rooms.

Right: *The house and gardens of Gaia House, Devon, England.*

Below: *The entrance to Gaia House.*

GAIA HOUSE

GAIA HOUSE IS IN THE PASTORAL LANDSCAPE OF south Devon, England. Founded in 1984 to provide an environment for the practice of insight meditation, Gaia House now offers a full year-round program of retreats, which includes weekends on other (mainly Buddhist) traditions. Its staff is drawn largely from the same international group of vipassana teachers who are to be found at IMS, together with people such as Martine and Stephen Batchelor who live locally (see Stephen's account of a three-month Zen retreat in the next section).

I went to a retreat at Gaia House three years ago. On the first morning, the five other men in my dormitory were all up at first light. I'll ease into it gently, I thought, turned over and went back to sleep. The next time I saw them was at breakfast, which was soon abbreviated by the gong for the next meditation session: forty-five minutes cross-legged on a meditation cushion, watching the rise and fall of my breath in the belly–when I wasn't drifting away on a daydream, that is, or preoccupied with the pain in my left knee. Then slow meditation

walking, one foot placed attentively in front of the other, in a circular procession around the room. Then back to the cushion for another round of daydreams punctuated with the odd moment of clarity and an intermittent stab in the knee. And so it went on, sitting and walking to lunch, and on again till dinner.

By the last meditation of that first day, there were already fewer shuffles and coughs in the silence. We were settling in, and I was aware of the clear space between one thought and the next.

I made it to the 6 o'clock session the next morning. I sat and slow-walked through the day, with no choice but to acknowledge my boredom and scattered attention. By the fifth day, though, I was finding it hard not to laugh. The person I thought I was–all the jumbled contents of my mind–I had seen to be like dust on the water. Behind or below my mind, a bright, silent awakeness had declared its existence–only sporadically, yes, but enough to give rise to a trust in life deeper than all doubts.

ZEN BUDDHISM

FROM THE PERSPECTIVE OF ZEN, INSIGHT INTO THE TRUE nature of existence can be had anywhere, at any moment, not only on a meditation cushion. Zen has traditionally seen less of a divide than Theravada between monastics and laity. It has cultivated the arts and crafts as a means of enlightenment as well as formal meditation practice; there are many Zen stories of a student being sent to work in the kitchens, or as a woodsman, for years, until he finally comes to the master and asks if he can receive the teachings. "What do you think you have been receiving for the last twenty years?" the teacher replies.

The Zen approach to meditation falls broadly into two schools, Rinzai and Soto, although in the West, the different forms are increasingly used in the same retreat. Rinzai Zen is dynamic; it centers round the asking of a question, or koan, by which the questioner can penetrate the truth of existence. The question is always one which defies reason; it has no answer, as such. The real nature of the practitioner is itself the answer and it can only be arrived at by being the answer. Koans which have entered the American vernacular to the point of becoming Zen clichés are, "What is the sound of one hand clapping?" or "What was your original face before you were born?" Such questions push the logical mind beyond paradox and duality.

The Rinzai school developed from the teaching style of Rinzai Gigen, a master in ninth century China. Soto Zen originated with Dogon Zenji, a master in thirteenth century Japan who emphasized that

Right: *Japanese Zen Buddhism
continues to be the most popular
form of Buddhism practiced in
America, where tradition and
authority are constantly
challenged.*

Previous pages:
*36. Thich Nhat Hanh, the
Buddhist leader, with his
disciples.*

*37. The Buddhist Wheel of Life,
from the facade of a temple at the
Swayambhunath in Katmandu.*

sitting practice was itself an expression of enlightenment. In Soto there is no goal, nowhere to go other than where you are now. There is no method, other than the non-effort of being here, eyes softly open, facing a white wall.

"The Soto way of "gradual awakening" contrasts with the Rinzai emphasis on "sudden enlightenment." According to Soto teachings, one takes a long, slow walk through the morning dew to realize the Buddhist ideal of getting thoroughly soaked by the rains of wisdom. The atmospheric conditions of Rinzai come closer to those of a flash flood." (Helen Tworkov, *Zen in America.*)

The Japanese schools of Zen first brought Buddhism to America. Zen continues to be the most popular form of American Buddhism, although Zen teachers from Vietnam, Korea and China now have many students in America and Europe as well. D T Suzuki, who died in 1966, became the popularized voice of Zen through his writings, which had a profound influence on some of the most creative minds of the century. John Cage, Eric Fromm, Aldous Huxley, Thomas Merton, Jung and many others took a great interest in Suzuki's expositions of Zen. It was through the influence of people like these, as well as through poets and writers like Alan Ginsberg, Gary Snyder, Jack Kerouac and Alan Watts, that Zen attracted so much attention in the fifties and sixties.

Since the eighties, the mystique of Zen has become somewhat neutralized and questions have emerged that would never have been asked in Japan. Traditionally, the conduct, moral or otherwise, of a teacher would never have been questioned and, as the embodiment of the

Left: *An American Theravada monk in Ladakh, India: the short period of American influence on Zen has revitalized the tradition, which existed unchanged for centuries.*

Opposite: *Work at the Insight Meditation Center. Similar practices occur at Rinzai Zen retreats.*

enlightened state, whatever he did could not be judged by normal moral codes. Any deviations from the ideal did not diminish his authority or the practitioners' dedication. In America, tradition and authority are constantly challenged; the scandals in various Zen centers in the USA have shown the value for Zen of bringing the questioning mind to bear upon even the conduct of the master himself. Americans are thus returning Zen to its earliest principles, which always place individual conscience and insight above received knowledge and authority. There is no doubt that in the "Western transmission" of the twentieth century, Zen is being revitalized in a way it had not known for centuries in its original homelands.

THREE-MONTH RINZAI ZEN RETREAT IN KOREA

"THE RETREAT BEGAN IN EARNEST THE FOLLOWING MORNING AT two. And this insane routine–thirteen hours of meditation ending at ten at night–was to continue for 89 more days. Fifty minutes seated on a cushion, followed by ten minutes walking briskly round the hall, each session measured by the tedious ticking of an ancient clock and the shocking cracks of a wooden clapper; such were the new parameters of my temporal world, interrupted only for food and insufficient sleep.

"The first two weeks were the worst. After that knees and mind became resigned and, imperceptibly, the routine switches from an outrageous exception to the very norm against which all else is understood... I am expected to ask with all my strength, "What is it?" Or "What is this?" or simply "What?" I am told that it is the questioning, the doubt, that matters, not the words."

"And so the moon swells and vanishes for three months while a small group of humans sit cross-legged on cushions struggling with an impossible question. By the mid-way point, it becomes hard to believe that I ever did anything else. Memories are just more of the same inner telex, clattering away to little effect. But as the tantalizing end of the retreat peeks over the horizon and draws nearer each day, restlessness begins to eat at you: plans are pulled out from the lockers of the subconscious mind and dusted off; bus schedules are contemplated; maybe a movie in the local town... The last week is probably worse than the first."

(Stephen Batchelor, *The Faith to Doubt.*)

THE CH'AN RETREAT AND MASTER SHENG YEN

Ch'AN IS THE ORIGINAL CHINESE FROM WHICH THE Japanese word Zen is derived. Master Sheng Yen conducts Ch'an retreats in New York and Taiwan and occasionally in Britain. He is Director of the Institute of Chung Hwa Buddhist Culture in Taipei, Taiwan and president of the same Institute in New York. The New York Institute runs the Ch'an Meditation Center, of which he is the master. He is also abbot of a monastery in Taipei.

A retreat with Sheng Yen is a period of intensive meditation training that usually lasts for seven days. Boards are struck at 4.00AM and physical exercises begin at 4.15PM. This is followed by three half-hour sittings before the morning liturgy is chanted. Breakfast follows in silence, which is kept for the entire retreat. Then there is an hour's work period, with each participant being allotted a task—washing up, bringing in logs, etc. Five sittings follow, between which, except for the last two, there are periods of standing yoga, sitting yoga, slow and fast walking. Lunch and another work period is followed by five further sittings with similar breaks until the evening chant. After supper, Master Sheng-Yen gives a talk at 7.00PM. Then there are three more sits, without break for exercise, and bed at 10.00PM. Apart from interviews with the master, no talking is allowed at any time.

Shih-fu, as the master is known in the Ch'an tradition, has the broad approach typical of Ch'an and recommends a variety of practices depending on the individual, with whom he discusses the choice of method in interview. He normally begins with counting the breath with awareness. He rarely mentions the word enlightenment and makes it quite clear that his retreats are for the development of practice. To Shih-fu, the purpose of the retreat is:

1. *To realize one is not in control of one's own mind*
2. *To discover how to train one's mind in awareness*
3. *To calm the mind*
4. *To provide opportunities for repentance and hence to regain immaculacy*
5. *To practice with an individually suitable method that will yield insight*

Left: *Whether walking, sleeping, eating or preparing food, the importance is to do it mindfully, to be aware of the process and one's stream of thought.*

Far left: *Master Sheng-Yen leading retreat at the Western Zen Center, followed closely by Dr. John Crook and other retreatants.*

"The personal interview is a key element in the contact between master and trainee. Shih-fu has the ability to assume many appearances. At interview he may appear remote, severe, totally detached and disinterested, even withering, waiting for you to produce something worthwhile and dismissing you when you don't. Or he may appear compassionate and caring while always returning the problem to the trainee... There may be silence or speech. There is always presence."

(John Crook, *Catching a Feather on a Fan*.)

In his book, *Getting the Buddha Mind,* Master Sheng-Yen includes some reports from people who have attended his retreats. One participant wrote the following:

"I had been working on the kung-an (koan) "Where am I?" I think it was the fourth day during a meditation period when I suddenly felt I was on the verge of some kind of understanding but I couldn't find any words for it. I let the feeling pass. Later that day I was in the kitchen cleaning the drinking glasses. Each person was assigned a specific glass solely for their use during the retreat. I picked up the first glass. My name was on it. I began to laugh. That's where Marina was, in the sink. I had no name. It was as if the way I perceived things was becoming a little looser, freer."

THE WESTERN ZEN RETREAT

A T HIS FARMHOUSE RETREAT CENTER IN REMOTE rural Wales, Dr. John Crook has developed a form of Zen practice designed for lay people who may have little interest in or experience of classical Buddhism but who have a keen interest in meditation as a means of discovering the workings of their own mind. In a five day retreat, the first two days will be given to zazen sitting, the next three to a communication exercise and the last day to zazen again. For the communication exercise, participants rotate in pairs and ask each other a variant of traditional koan questions, like, "Tell me who you are." The questioner hears the responses in silence for five minutes and then exchanges roles with his partner. The retreat leader keeps time with a gong. The day begins around 6.00AM and ends at 10.30PM. Each person has an interview with the retreat leader.

Dr. John Crook is Reader in Ethology at the Department of Psychology at Bristol University, UK. He has had long training in various Zen, as well as Tibetan, schools of meditation and has received the Dharma transmission from Master Sheng Yen, entitling him to conduct Ch'an retreats.

THICH NHAT HANH AND PLUM VILLAGE

THICH NHAT HANH IS A VIETNAMESE ZEN BUDDHIST master who came to the West during the Vietnam war. He made it the practice of his monks and nuns to pick up the dead and wounded in the streets of Saigon and carry them to safety, breathing with mindfulness as they did so. Tai, as he is known, is an engaged Buddhist; his teachings are as much about one's relationship and regard for the environment and other people as they are about meditation.

He has had a significant influence on the American Buddhist community in the last ten years, introducing a softer, more "feminine" approach to Zen practice and to the Buddhist perspective in general. More than just being, he emphasizes what he calls "inter-being," being-in-relationship. It is for this reason that Plum Village, his residence and Zen Community in the south of France, runs family retreats every summer. I went on one of these retreats with my family in 1990.

Below: *Walking meditation at Spirit Rock, Plum Village.*

Right: *The Shuso ceremony, or Head Student empowerment, at a Buddhist spiritual gathering.*

We pitched our tents near the renovated farmhouse and joined the queue for dinner. A group of people were chanting under a tree; others were filing out of the meditation hall; some children were playing with kites. The first thing that struck me was that people seemed to be enjoying themselves. Buddhist retreats are usually a serious affair: people rarely smile, or even look at each other but here, participants made a point of greeting you warmly. In the dinner queue I asked someone when the next meditation session was.

"Sometime tomorrow morning," came the reply.

Mediation, Tai told us in one of his daily talks, is a matter of quality, not quantity. It is an openness, a spaciousness of mind that one can practice anywhere and in the company of anyone. It should not be restricted to the meditation hall; and even in formal practice, it helps to have a slight smile on one's face. I discovered in the following days how much that smile helps to dissolve the tendency to take oneself and one's efforts so seriously.

All of us, children and adults, were introduced to the pleasure of

meditation, "Plum Village style." Instead of a step-by-step procession with each person attentive to themselves alone, Tai encouraged us to walk together, moving mindfully, taking in the beauty of the countryside; even holding hands. The point was to experience the reality of our inter-being with others, with nature, and with the earth.

Everything else we did that week had an element of the same intention. There were tea ceremonies, in which small groups gathered quietly round a tray of tea and biscuits, shared in a silence broken only when someone needed to express something deeply felt, as in a Quaker meeting. There was singing, silent painting sessions, where we all worked together on a long scroll of paper; mediation sessions, and talks by Tai on Buddhist texts. By the end of the week my whole family had relaxed more into the present moment and knew our inter-being to be a fact of existence.

Most of Tai's retreats are run in the same informal manner, and children are generally welcome. He teaches throughout Europe and the USA, and also runs occasional retreats exclusively for Vietnam veterans.

THE SONOMA MOUNTAIN ZEN CENTER

THE SPIRITUAL HEAD OF THIS ZEN CENTER IS THE CHINESE American master, Jakusho Kwong Roshi, who continues the Soto Zen lineage of Shunryu Suzuki-Roshi, the founder of the San Francisco Zen Center. According to Kwong, Buddhist teachings are only now beginning to enter the United States. To cultivate the American Buddha fields, he says, requires confusion, change and even deep despair. "The first two decades of Zen in America were about the meeting of Japanese and American cultures. Because we were so new to the form, we leaned on our teachers, projected everything onto them and in some ways lost our center point." Then, laughing, he adds: "It's always just beginning. Everything is always just beginning."

"I am trying to be more experimental," he continues. "I am trying to find out what works. With confidence and maturity, I was able to give up my attachment to the Soto Zen form, to doing things as close to the way Suzuki Roshi did them. What is the form? No one has the answer. I used to think that some other teachers had the "right" answer or had the "right" form. Now I know we are all in the same boat, trying to keep these teachings alive in this aggressive land of confusion."
(Helen Tworkov, *Zen in America*.)

The Sonoma Mountain Zen Center was founded in 1974 and is situated on eighty acres of rolling hills and mountainous land. The sangha is a small community of single students and families, joined by a large number of practitioners for various set retreats. The Center offers meditation instruction and guest retreats throughout the year. There is a month-long guest practice retreat in July. The community has a commitment to daily zazen practice.

TIBETAN BUDDHISM

THE TIBETAN DIASPORA OF THE LAST THIRTY years is tragic for Tibet and Tibetan culture as a whole; yet no-one can deny the immense benefit that the Western world has received from the dissemination of this unique culture of wisdom and spirituality. A tradition jealously guarded behind mountains and monastery walls for centuries has now become available through a formidable array of schools, retreat centers and universities throughout Europe and America. Great lamas and rinpoches have given, and continue to give, their empowerments and initiations to thousands of students throughout the Western world.

As in the case of Japanese Zen, the movement westwards has undoubtedly benefited the Tibetan traditions themselves which, by the time the Chinese invaded Lhasa in the fifties, were beginning to suffer the inevitable degeneration that accompanies prolonged insularity and unchallenged hierarchy. Some great lamas found the challenges of Western society difficult to adapt to and, like some of the Zen masters, experienced inevitable friction between their assumed inviolable

Right: *Gomba Thiksey, the beautiful monastery of the Tibetan community at Ladakh, India.*

Previous pages:
48 (top). The entrance to Kanying Gonba, Nepal.

48 (bottom). A Tibetan monk in exile in India celebrates his faith.

49. Tibetan monks call others to prayer in their temple.

authority and the questioning of a culture that did not accept transgression of its own ethical and moral codes. The traditions of Tibet have had to adapt to their new environment and have shed some of their more outworn attitudes as a result.

The three principal schools of Tibetan Buddhism are the Kagyu, the Nyingma and the Gelug. The Kagyu school traces its lineage back to the great Indian master, Naropa; among its basic teachings are the "Six Yogas of Naropa," which include mystic heat (dumo), yoga and the yoga of the bardo, the intermediate state between death and rebirth. These disciplines are known as particularly fast routes to buddhahood but they have to be practiced with great energy, under the guidance of a qualified master.

The broad emphasis of the Kagyu school is on practical mysticism, rather than on scholarship. Along with other tantric traditions, it does not require strict celibacy or membership of a religious institution, though as it developed it did start its own monasteries, like other Tibetan schools. In the course of time the Kagyu divided into various sub-sects, the best known of which today is the Karma Kagyu. The head of this sect is known as the Karmapa, who is considered to reincarnate into a fresh body on the demise of his previous one. When he dies, he leaves behind a letter containing directions and a search is then begun for the child who embodies the compassionate spirit which is the mark of all Karmapas. This is a common system in many Tibetan lineages: beings who are identified as reincarnations of a previous master are known as tulku and carry the title Rinpoche ("precious one").

The sixteenth Karmapa died in Chicago in 1981 and his reincarnation was only discovered some ten years later; a child of a nomadic family in Tibet. The sixteenth Karmapa was one of the first to appreciate the importance of disseminating the teachings to Westerners and he sent lamas to the West early on. One of them, Chogyam Trungpa (1939-1987) established the first Tibetan center in Scotland, Samye Ling, then went on to America, where he founded the Naropa Institute in Boulder, Colorado, which is now a full university specializing in Buddhist Studies.

The Nyingma school distinguishes nine paths to Enlightenment, the first three being based on the sutras and the remaining six on the tantras. It traces its lineage to Padmasambhava (guru rinpoche), the tantric adept who arrived in Tibet in the eighth century, who alone possessed the occult powers necessary to turn the demon and spirit religion of Tibet to the way of Buddha.

The Nyingmapa are the most individualistic, least hierarchically organized of the Tibetan traditions. Their lamas, or spiritual teachers, were often married men who operated independently in Tibet at a local level. Many of them supported themselves by dispensing occult services—exorcism, rainmaking, divination, healing, etc.—that the ordinary Tibetan required. They are still known as ngakpas. The school has produced many great adepts and masters who continue to be strongly in evidence today; the last supreme head of the order, H. H. Dudjom Rinpoche, established an important center in France where he died in 1987. One of his best known lamas is Sogyal Rinpoche, author of *The Tibetan Book of Living and Dying*.

Right: *Dalai Lama monks at prayer.*

Below: *A portrait of one of the earliest Dalai Lamas.*

Left: *The Dalai Lama talks to his followers at their temple in Dharamsala.*

The founder of the Gelug school was Tsongkhapa, who lived from 1357 to 1419. Identified as a manifestation of Manjushri, Boddhisattva of Wisdom, Tsongkhapa founded three of the largest monasteries in Tibet: Ganden, Drepung and Sera. Because of their scholarly orientations and their division into colleges, they are often known as monastic universities.

Tsongkhapa was a reformer who reaffirmed the importance of monastic virtues and the need to establish a firm basis in the sutra (scriptural) teachings before graduating to the tantras. He defined the path to Enlightenment as a series of stages, which he expounded in a famous text known as *Lam Rim Chenmo*.

From among his disciples came the line of Dalai Lamas. The word Dalai is of Mongolian origin and means "ocean," implying an ocean or vast repository of wisdom. The title of Dalai Lama was bestowed posthumously on Gendun-drup, a direct disciple of Tsongkhapa. When the Mongol Khans began to favor the Gelug school, the fifth Dalai Lama became virtual head of all Tibet under Mongol protection. From that time, the Dalai Lama has been considered both the secular and the spiritual head of Tibet, as well as the head of the Gelug school.

In all forms of Tibetan Buddhism, the lama is considered essential if the disciple is to deal successfully with the difficulties of the spiritual path. The meditation techniques and initiations the lama may give a practitioner will vary widely according both to lineage and individual predilections. They might include creative visualization, symbolic teachings, mantra, yoga, techniques of bare attention similar to Soto Zen, guru devotion and personal transmission.

The overall tantric approach to Buddhist practice that typifies Tibetan traditions is called Vajrayana, which is "supposed to be not merely psychologically but also magically effective, employing devastating and irresistible techniques to destroy the ego... The principal distinction between Vajrayana and other forms of Mahayana is its emphasis on transmutation–as opposed to destruction–of neurosis. Where other approaches to Buddhist meditation seek to destroy passion, aggression and ignorance so that the practitioner can be free from ego-clinging, Vajrayana seeks to transform the three poisons directly into wisdom, actually transmuting the constituents of the ego directly into principles of Buddhahood."

(Don Morreale, *Buddhist America*.)

THE NYINGMA INSTITUTE

THE PRINCIPAL CENTER OF THE INSTITUTE IS IN BERKELEY, California. It exists for the study and practice of the teachings of Tarthang Tulku. There are meditation rooms, a library, bookstore and meditation garden. The Institute offers classes, seminars and long-term retreats and states that the Nyingma teachings offer keys for living a meaningful life in a contemporary world.

Left: Sogyal Rinpoche at a Rigpa retreat in Grenoble.

Right: The Sakya monks from Raspur dance the traditional Black Hat dance at Rigpa UK.

RIGPA

RIGPA IS THE WORLD-WIDE ORGANIZATION WHICH MAKES available the Nyingma teachings of Sogyal Rinpoche. Sogyal was raised in Tibet by one the country's greatest teachers, Khyentse Rinpoche. He came to England in 1971 to study Comparative Religion at Oxford. His life's work is to bridge East and West and to make the Buddhist teachings available everywhere. In 1993, his book *The Tibetan Book of Living and Dying* became a best seller in the USA and in Europe. He spent 1994 in personal retreat, only coming out to lead a few selected retreats for his students. One of these, called "Deepening the View," was held in England. Julia Desch was one of the retreatants and she had this to say about her experience:

"The Big Hall at Harrow, one of England's oldest fee-paying schools, had been transformed into a shrine-mediation room for the ten-day retreat. Tibetan mandalas (tangkas) hung all round the room, meditation cushions lined the floor, incense sweetened the air. Two hundred and fifty retreatants filled the hall.

"We spent most of the first three days in Dzogchen practice; short meditation sessions, watching our sensations and thoughts, eyes open. We would sit for ten minutes, then stand and stretch, sit for another ten minutes, and so on for an hour. Then we would break for a while, and start again. Some days one of the senior students would give a reading, and we would just sit in the inspiration of that. We also did TongLen practice, the Cultivation of Opening the Heart,

which took various forms—the practice of loving kindness towards oneself, towards friends and enemies, and towards the dying. There were also periods of prayer and prostrations.

"On the fourth day, Rinpoche arrived and gave a couple of hours teaching, which he did at the end of every following day until the end of the retreat. We formed into study groups to discuss the teachings and formulate questions, and also to help foster a sense of the sangha, the spiritual community.

"One of the things I love about a Tibetan retreat is that nothing is left out. In the middle of the retreat we had a sumptuous feast, including meat, accompanied by a long series of prayers and invocations. This was a Tibetan ritual for purifying mind, body, and

speech, which symbolically included the whole of creation in the process of transformation. Rather as in Holy Communion, the food was raised up alchemically, transformation being understood as a cellular process which included the whole body. Appropriately, the evening ended with joyous dancing.

"Throughout all his teachings, Rinpoche constantly emphasized the importance of practice in every shape and form, and the flow there needed to be between prayer, practice, and daily life. He urged us to nurture the inspiration we drew from the retreat, and to practice till we became an inspiration for others. That, he said, with one of his infectious laughs, is how people change and the transmission takes place."

LERAB LING

IN 1991, RIGPA EUROPE BOUGHT 359 ACRES OF WOODLAND AND meadows north of Montpellier, in an unspoiled area of southern France, to serve as a new retreat facility. They named the new center Lerab Ling, which means "sanctuary," or "place of enlightened action." It is already one of Europe's major retreat centers, and a number of retreats have already been held to explore the parallels between psychology, healing, and the traditional wisdom of Tibet. Sogyal Rinpoche intends to spend several months a year at Lerab Ling, giving spiritual training to his students. Other eminent masters from different streams of Buddhism will also run retreats at the center, and His Holiness. the Dalai Lama has been invited to run a special retreat there in 1995.

A conference hall/temple is being constructed in a revolutionary design that blends elements of Tibetan, Japanese, and Western styles, with glass walls on all sides. A children's village is being constructed that will enable parents to attend retreats.

DZOGCHEN BEARA

THIS RIGPA RETREAT CENTER IN SOUTH WEST IRELAND IS IDEAL for personal and solitary retreats, as well as the small group retreats it offers on its own program. It clings to the remote and spectacular coastline of the Beara Peninsula, looking out over the North Atlantic. Recent retreats have included sessions on healing and Tibetan medicine.

HOLY ISLAND RETREAT CENTER

THE FIRST OF ALL THE TIBETAN CENTERS IN THE WEST WAS Samye Ling in south-west Scotland, founded in 1967 by Chogyam Trungpa and Akong Tulku Rinpoche. In its first ten years many great masters taught there, including the sixteenth Karmapa and Kalu Rinpoche. In 1980 the center began the ten year training program, which is organized round the three year cloistered retreat and in 1992 it began a whole new phase of its development with the purchase of Holy Island, off the coast of western Scotland. Lama Yeshe, the retreat master of Samye Ling, is the Director of the Holy Island Project, one of Tibetan Buddhism's most ambitious and forward-looking projects in the western world.

Holy Island has spiritual connections stretching back to the sixth century, when Saint Laisren chose to retreat there, having spurned the throne of Ulster. With the acquisition of such a historic site, the Samye Ling community has attracted considerable national and international publicity. Other faiths in the area have expressed their approval of the project; the bishop of Saint Andrews wrote in the *Samye Ling Magazine* that he believes "the purchase of Holy Island and the imaginative invitation by the community to other faiths to share in the life of prayer which is planned for the island is a major step forward in the spiritual life of Scotland."

Left (top): *Holy Island, the dramatic Scottish setting for Samye Ling interfaith and Buddhist retreats.*

Left (below): *Views of the Dzogchen Beara Rigpa retreat center which overlooks the North Atlantic.*

Right: *The Buddhist Temple of Samye Ling, built by the community there.*

Following page: *An interfaith gathering on Holy Island.*

One of the first steps of the new owners was to hold an interfaith service on the island. Lama Yeshe plans to construct an Interfaith Retreat Center as well as the Buddhist Retreat Center. Another way visitors can share in the vision there is to take part in the environmental project; much of the land remains to be cleared and a tree planting project is in operation. The peaceful coexistence between mankind and nature is inherent to Buddhist teachings and working on Holy Island is a means of practicing this in a intentional way. The ecological revitalization of Holy Island is part of the Interfaith project, since it provides a common goal for people of different traditions to work towards. A conservation management plan for the island is now being put into action with the help of visiting volunteers from all over the world.

This account from Elizabeth Davies of Sussex University gives an idea of what a "conservation retreat" is like.

"We took the boat ride from Lamlash to Holy Island and I recognized it at once as the spiritual sanctuary of my dreams. Many of the group had no previous connection with Samye Ling or with Tibetan Buddhism but had been drawn by the nature of the Project. Our brief was to construct a dry stone wall, rhododendron control and beach clearing. We followed an almost monastic routine, rising at 6.00AM to the sound of a gong for a period of optional meditation, followed by breakfast, then work until lunch at 12.30PM. Then on after lunch until 6.00PM. There were many visitors to the Island during our stay and all were warmly welcomed. There always seemed enough food to go round and although the conditions were primitive and the weather often inclement, we managed well. For recreation we told stories, sang, walked with the goats and swam with the seals.

"We left the Island feeling inwardly and outwardly replenished, hoping to return next year and with a strong sense of some deeper underlying purpose to this new alliance between ancient Christianity and Tibetan Buddhism."

Holy Island is also a Tibetan Buddhist Retreat Center. Samye Ling is soon to move its three year retreat program to the Island (the three year retreat is described in the section, Solitary Retreats). It also offers

a general retreat program and accommodation for individual retreatants, who are free to decide how to arrange their day and do not need to be Buddhists. There are various meditation retreats available, though a Kagyu retreat can be tough: up to thirteen hours of meditation a day, seven days a week–the Kagyu tradition, after all, has been renowned for centuries for its instruction in meditation. And what is the benefit of it all? Retreat Master Lama Yeshe says, "If I am steady in my practice, the benefit will be a stable mind... if I have a stable mind I will have clarity so that my actions will never be a cause of suffering to other people." (*Samye Ling Magazine*.) The central teaching of the Kagyu, like that of all the other Mahayana Buddhist schools, is the practice of compassion. Meditation is for that–not for yourself but for the benefit of all beings.

Present retreat facilities are in the existing farmhouse and the old lighthouse station cottages, which are being renovated. An architectural competition to design a new monastery on the Island has just been won by an Amsterdam partnership from among two hundred entries by architects from all over Europe. The Dutch partners' scheme was the unanimous winner, having come up with an "elegant minimalist solution" which allows the wild and elemental landscape to remain the main feature. *The Scotsman* newspaper commented that "it will certainly prove to be the most outstanding piece of modern architecture to have been erected in Scotland for half a century and a masterpiece of ecclesiastical building by any standards."

RAJA YOGA

RAJA, OR ROYAL, YOGA, IS AN INTRICATE SYSTEM OF PRACTICES whose original philosophical source is the classical Sanskrit text, *The Yoga Sutras*, composed by Patanjali some time in the first or second century CE. Raja Yoga consists of a way of life designed to enable the practitioner to see through the illusion of created existence and to become established in his existential identity. The first four of Patanjali's sutras give the essence of what this yoga is.

"The discipline of Yoga is that state of being in which the choice-making movement of the mind slows down and comes to a stop. Then, the seer gets established in his existential identity. In all other states of being, identification with the ideational, choice-making movement reigns supreme." (P. D. Deshpande, *The Authentic Yoga*.)

The purpose of Raja Yoga, then, is ultimately to move beyond the duality caused by identification with thought, to the unified condition in which there is no gap between the seen and the one who sees–which is known in Sanskrit and in English as samadhi. Traditional Raja Yoga, however, is a gradual path of ascent which includes practices for every level of being, from the physical through the moral and ethical to the deepest levels of meditation. The sutras describe this path as The Eight Petalled Flower of Yoga, which includes moral qualities such as non-violence and truthfulness, asana–the training of the body through posture (hatha yoga)–pranayama, the control of the breath and progressively deeper degrees of absorption into stillness, culminating in sahaj samadhi, known as the natural state of non-differentiation. The aim of Raja Yoga is not to transform the mind, more to transcend it altogether.

THE SELF-REALIZATION FELLOWSHIP

"THE PURPOSE OF THE SELF-Realization Fellowship Retreat is to help you feel an awareness of the indwelling Spirit, which resides in every man. The scriptures of all religions declare man to be made in the image of God; the testimony of all the saints is that in this divine image within lies the fulfillment, the joy, the love our hearts seek.

You may have come on retreat to rest and to find inspiration and spiritual renewal. Or you may be seeking answers to questions or solutions to problems that can be resolved only by deep reflection, understanding and inner guidance. Whatever you have come for, the success of your endeavor rests ultimately on the personal relationship you have with God... the Source of life, wisdom... happiness. In the measure you cultivate awareness of His indwelling Presence, you will receive inspiration and assurance and guidance towards solving every problem in life." (The Self-Realization Fellowship, *A Retreatant's Companion*.)

The Self-Realization Fellowship was founded in the United States in the twenties by Paramahansa Yogananda, one of the earliest exponents of Raja Yoga in the West and author of the classic spiritual work, *Autobiography of a Yogi*. He arrived in America in 1920 as a delegate to an international congress of religious leaders in Boston and was an immediate success among American intellectuals and seekers of his day. He conveyed the authority of a living, highly sophisticated system of Raja Yoga in terms that suited the scientific mood of the time. He taught a carefully graded system of energization, concentration and meditation techniques, that still serve as the substance of the Fellowship's teachings today.

However, as the quotation shows, Yogananda's approach was not limited to mind or energy control. The importance of a devotional and personal relationship with God is central in all his teachings, another reminder of how much the various ways overlap. Raja Yoga draws on all the different yogas, including bhakti (devotion) yoga and karma yoga (the way of action in the world).

After a minimum of a year of practice with energization and concentration techniques, the Fellowship student may continue with

Right: *The Self-Realization Fellowship retreat center, Los Angeles.*

Left: *The meditation building, known as the Lake Shrine, in the gardens of the Self-Realization Fellowship, Los Angeles.*

Kriya Yoga, a system of meditation particular to Yogananda, "which reinforces and revitalizes subtle currents of life energy in the body, enabling the normal activities of heart and lungs to slow down naturally. As a result, the consciousness is drawn to higher levels of perception, gradually bringing about an inner awakening more blissful... than any of the experiences that the mind or the senses or the ordinary human emotions can give." (The Self-Realization Fellowship, *An Introduction to Self-Realization*.)

To take up the Kriya Yoga practice also signifies the establishment of a personal bond between the disciple and the guru, Yogananda himself.

The Fellowship today is a world-wide network coordinated and led by a monastic order, with more than four hundred centers and several retreat facilities–including the one established in 1936 by Yogananda in Encinitas, one hundred miles south of Los Angeles, with headquarters in Los Angeles itself. Local centers meet all over the

world for the practice of meditation and to give a sense of community and support to those who follow the Self-Realization Fellowship teachings by post through a series of home study lessons. The Self-Realization Retreat in Encinitas runs its own retreat program and is available for students and for sincere seekers to stay for up to two weeks. Another retreat center, Hidden Valley, near Escondido, California, offers programs specifically for men, including a work-retreat, through which participants may join the resident monks in their daily schedule.

The Self-Realization Fellowship monks and nuns also conduct retreats several times a year elsewhere in the US and abroad. A Self-Realization Fellowship retreat will involve classes on Yogananda's teachings, energization exercises, group meditation, chanting, devotional services and support from the company of others of like mind. The retreats are held in silence.

THE BRAHMA KUMARIS WORLD SPIRITUAL UNIVERSITY

THE BRAHMA KUMARIS ARE ONE OF THE SPIRITUAL MOVEMENTS in the world today that are truly international and non-denominational. They do not preach any specific religious philosophy, they are not a sect nor do they have a mission. Instead of requiring belief, their spiritual teachings are verified by the practitioner through personal experience. Though their practices and approach to life are founded in Raja Yoga, the term is not mentioned anywhere in their public literature. They speak directly to Western needs and concerns, emphasizing the value of meditation and concentration techniques for dealing more effectively with the challenges of everyday life.

The movement started in Karachi with the vision and energy of one man, Dada Lekhraj. In 1936, after building a successful diamond business, Dada began to devote more and more time to deep contemplation, which led to a series of visionary experiences. At the age of sixty, he dedicated the rest of his life and all his wealth to establishing a University which would teach people spiritual principles and practices and how to apply them in the everyday life. He discouraged any perception that would label him as a guru and directed everyone's attention instead to the Supreme, whom he recognized as the primary inspiration for the University and its work.

For fourteen years, the founding group of three hundred people lived in a self-sufficient community, spending their time in intense spiritual study, meditation and self transformation. Then in 1951 the community moved to Mount Abu, in Rajasthan, India, to what is now their International Headquarters. By 1969, when Dada died, there were over four hundred centers in India. Now there are over three thousand centers in sixty-two countries, each offering courses, workshops and conferences on a whole range of topics including self development, cooperative and communication skills and meditation.

Right: *Devotees gather in the main hall of the Brahma Kumaris University Global Retreat Center, watched over by a portrait of the group's founder, Dada Lekhraj.*

Left: *The Brahma Kumaris World Spiritual University Global Retreat Center, Nuneham Park.*

Since Karma Yoga, the practice of spiritual principles in the world, is an integral part of Raja Yoga, the Brahma Kumaris contribute to the work of community centers, prisons, hospitals and schools and operate a Global Hospital Project for the local population at Mount Abu. They also organize international events such as the annual Universal Peace Conference and the Global Cooperation for a Better World Project which was launched in 1988 at The United Nations Headquarters in New York.

Retreats are organized by local centers, at the Retreat Center at Mount Abu and at their recently-opened Global Retreat Center at Nuneham Park, an eighteenth century stately home near Oxford. They are normally run over a long weekend by the staff of the Center, who are all meditation teachers. They aim to provide busy people with a quiet period in a nourishing and beautiful atmosphere, in which they can explore and sustain their own personal spiritual experience. The teachers provide guidance in meditation, an outline of spiritual principles and discussion sessions on themes like "Spirituality in Daily Life." All the retreats are free of charge.

SHAMANISM
KNOWLEDGE THROUGH RITUAL

UNTIL THE POPULAR CIRCULATION OF CARLOS CASTANEDA'S books, beginning in 1967 with The Teachings of Don Juan, the word "shaman" was barely known, much less understood. Now, especially in North America, it is part of the vernacular to the degree that even a pop group can call themselves The Shamen.

Whether or not those associations would meet with the approval of a traditional shaman is another matter. The word comes from the language of the Tungus tribe in Siberia; shamanism was once a world-wide tradition which reflected the intimate connection between tribal peoples and nature. Today, it is most alive in its original form in parts of Asia and in the Americas. Don Juan, the hero in Castaneda's books, lived the life of an ordinary Mexican whilst pursuing the "way of knowledge" in the ancient manner of secret transmission from teacher to pupil. The transmission was carried out through a long apprenticeship and the knowledge and power he gained were expressions of that culture's world view and its traditions.

The knowledge a shaman acquires reflects his underlying belief systems about the world and his place in it, just as anyone else's knowledge will reflect their own priorities and beliefs. Shamanistic knowledge has a somewhat different slant to the knowledge acquired by a Buddhist or a yogi. The latter aim to see through the illusory nature of all phenomena and ultimately through the mirage of their own identity, in order to realize their identity with all things. A shaman learns to see the objective world as just one of various possible worlds: there is also the subjective world, in which all things are connected; the symbolic world, in which everything has layers of meaning; and the world of being, of existential oneness with all things.

Left: *A modern shamanistic drum, used for ritual and spiritual exploration.*

Far left: *Like many ancient traditions, shamanism holds ceremonies for initiation into the practice.*

His purpose in knowing these worlds is to be able to travel freely through them with absolute control. The shaman is a shape-shifter moving between worlds at will and communicating with the different beings of the various realms. Unlike the channeler, who becomes possessed by a spirit from a different world, the shaman goes to meet the spirits in their own domain. Don Juan told Castaneda that the characteristics of a shaman were "joy, efficiency and abandonment in the face of all odds."

The shaman gains knowledge of the other worlds in order to be effective in this one and recreates himself according to his knowledge of these subtler worlds. He is a spiritual warrior, whose allies and teachers lie as much in the spiritual domains as in this one. One of his or her tasks is to find a spirit guide. In an essay in which she speaks to a river, Rowena Pattee asks how the guide might be found. The river replies,

"By invoking a spirit-guide, by clarifying your intention and by releasing the last stronghold on your fixed self-images. Open to the great world of spirit. The Sky is the spirit. Yet spirit is in all of nature. There is no place the spirit does not go." (Gary Doore, *Shaman's Path*.)

The principal way for the shaman to enter other worlds is by way of ritual involving the drum, rattle, dance and sometimes psychoactive drugs. The shaman replaces the solitude, silence and immobility of the yogi with rituals which use repetitive sound and movement in order to generate trance states to propel him into the world of spirits and power animals, gods and guardians.

In contemporary America and Europe, neoshamanism offers a spiritual path which is proving attractive to many people for a variety of reasons. Shamanism proper is difficult to come across not only because tribal cultures everywhere are in a decline but also because of the secrecy which surrounds the teachings. Even if a Westerner does come across a genuine shaman in his own tribal context, few are willing to undergo the long, arduous apprenticeship of a Castaneda.

Neoshamanism is the result of the meeting between Shamanistic teachings and Western culture. The teachers themselves have either been raised in a Western context, or have had long exposure to it. Their teachings are tailored to the needs and the conditioning of their Western audience, who like results and quickly; having been raised in

Below: *A bird's understanding of the natural world is vastly different from our own and a shaman endeavors to experience this alternative reality.*

Right: *The shaman enters other worlds through ritual involving dance, rattle and drum.*

a culture that gives overwhelming credence to the objective world, we are fascinated by the alternate realities that Shamanistic ritual can lead us into.

Neoshamanism is making a small but important contribution to the revival of spirituality in the West. Like any other tradition it has its charlatans but there are now a number of highly respected teachers in the USA whose practices have become part of a way of life for many people. Neoshamanism does not work within the framework of the tribal society. It primarily addresses well-educated, middle-class, predominantly white people; instead of putting forward the practices of a specific tribe, it blends teachings from societies around the world with Western psychology. Whereas in traditional Shamanistic societies very few people aspire to become shamans, within Shamanistic retreats everyone aspires to a state of transcendence in order to heal themselves and others.

Michael Harner, Director of The Foundation for Shamanic Studies, speaks for many when he counters criticisms of Shamanistic "crash courses" by saying,

"If the nation states of the world are working day and night on a crash course of their own for our mutual annihilation, we cannot afford to be any slower in our work in the opposite direction. The leisurely teaching that was possible in ancient tribal cultures is no longer appropriate. The forces of nuclear and ecological destruction are in a hurry and we must be too. People... need to be awakened not just through ordinary reality education, however important it is, but also through personal, heartfelt spiritual realization—deep realization of the connectedness of all things. May we work together and as fast as we can." (*Newsletter*, The Foundation for Shamanic Studies.)

A Shamanistic retreat revolves around ritual. It is a retreat in the real sense: participants are not only taking themselves away from their habitual life and activities for a weekend, a week, or more, they are leaving the objective world of concrete reality to enter the alternate state of the shaman. Two well-known ceremonies, the Sweatlodge and the Sundance, are described below by participants. There is also a description of the retreats run by a Kahuna shaman from Hawaii, Serge King.

THE SUNDANCE CEREMONY

"IN 1987 I WENT TO MY FIRST SUNDANCE, THE NATIVE AMERICAN Annual ceremony of renewal. I had joined the Deer Tribe the previous autumn and heard SwiftDeer, leader and chief teacher, say that all apprentices are expected to go to the Sundance. I had read Black Elk and Lame Deer and I wanted to receive a vision of my Sacred Dream. I really had very little idea what I was in for. I had my long, fringed skirts and ribbon shirts, my eagle whistle and plumes, my first shield and many give-aways.

"The Sundance involves a week of hard preparation building the arbor, a huge circle of poles entirely enclosed with brush to a height of about fifteen feet. The temperature was in the nineties and despite having my period, I was determined to do my bit and work as hard as anyone else, cutting small trees, hauling them to the trucks, unloading and stacking them around the arbor. By the time the Sundance started, one twilight a week later, I was exhausted. Nevertheless, as over a hundred dancers walked solemnly in pairs around the outside of the arbor to the slow beat of a huge drum, shivers ran up and down my spine with the echoes of having done this before a long time ago and there was a joy in me to be part of such an ancient, powerful, collective ceremony.

"We filed in and each took our place around the circumference where we had a narrow sleeping and resting place under the sloping brush.

The drumming and chanting began and I started to dance. I found the dance very difficult; each dancer has a "lane" from their place on the circle to the central Tree. They dance to the tree with their intent or prayer and then dance backwards in the same lane, receiving the power from the Tree. No-one ever turns their back on the Tree. In my naive enthusiasm that first night, I ran to the Tree as fast as I could and staggered backwards. Finally at 2.00AM the drum and singing ceased for the night. Exhausted, I collapsed into my sleeping bag.

"At 6.00AM the next morning the drum began again. Stiff and aching, I began to dance again, more slowly this time, trying through the protests of my body to feel the energy of the Tree and the drum, to open myself to Spirit and to vision. As the day wore on, I discovered that my assigned place in the north-east received full sun almost all day. Others, better prepared than me, had sheets that they strung up across their resting place to provide some shade. The sun was relentless. I spent increasing amounts of time lying down, crying at times with frustration. I had come all this way, thousands of miles, to dance and I could only lie there and groan. It never occurred to me to ask for help from the healing team. I hung on somehow until, after three days, the dance finally ended and we spent two days clearing up and returning the land to its original state.

"Two years later, I decided to go again, forewarned and forearmed. I found a friendly bunch from Michigan who took me in and shared cooking equipment and friendship. I took easier preparation jobs. I was placed in the south-west, the place of the Dream. I danced more gently, more fluidly and began to be able at times to let go of my thoughts and let the rhythm of the ceremony carry me.

"Towards the end of the second day, it was time for us to paint ourselves with our power in order to dance our shields to the Tree to

awaken them. I painted my face and hands and then had the inspiration to paint lightning bolts on my feet coming up from my toes, to represent Spirit coming in with energy to dance. I danced easily for the remainder of the Sundance. I moved into another space, finally open to the tremendous energy of the ceremony, finally surrendering and not trying to do it all myself. I felt I was beginning to gain a glimpse of what this ceremony might mean. I took this awareness into my fourth Sundance two years later. This Sundance was held in high desert, so the environmental conditions were even tougher. I took very good care of myself beforehand and dancing the first night, went each time to the Tree with the offering of myself exactly as I was, with no thought of trying to be anything else. I was dancing from the West towards the open gate and altars in the East and felt the deep joy of self-acceptance, the vital step for connecting with my Child Spirit Shield. I still encountered difficulties during the long three days but I knew I was only experiencing old "stuff" that was gradually passing. Many times, the beauty and energy of the singing and drumming, the clarity of the air and the power of Grandmother Earth beneath my feet took me into a knowing of my connection with all beings. I knew Harmony and Balance. My journey continues." Carol Youngson-White Owl.

Carol Youngson-White Owl took part in the Sweet Medicine Sundances organized by The Deer Tribe Metis Medicine Society. The Deer Tribe was founded by Harley SwiftDeer Reagan in the late 1970s. SwiftDeer is known internationally as a psychologist, philosopher, shaman and healer. He began his medicine apprenticeship at the age of eight with his Cherokee Grandmother Spotted Fawn and his teaching work now blends Western and Shamanic influences.

Right: *The ritual of dance forces the consciousness to leave every-day preoccupations and to focus instead on new and different layers of reality.*

Left: *The shaman enters the reality of spirits and power animals to achieve greater harmony with the surrounding world.*

THE SWEATLODGE CEREMONY:

AN ACCOUNT BY LEO RUTHERFORD

"THE SWEATLODGE IS PROBABLY THE EARLIEST MEANS OF cleansing that humanity has devised. Through the ceremony of the Sweatlodge one is purified at all levels of one's being. While the sauna is derivative of the ancient Scandinavian peoples, the most familiar Sweatlodge is in the style of the Native American people. It is used in contemporary culture today either on its own, as a purification ritual normally lasting a day and a night, or as the culminating part of a longer ceremony. I have been asked many times by people who have never entered a Sweatlodge, "What is the difference between a sauna and a Sweatlodge ceremony?" My answer is always the same: there is no similarity between the two except for heat and sweat.

"The lodge is constructed out of saplings bent and tied together to form an igloo shape. It is then covered with old blankets, tarpaulins and whatever is available until it is dark inside. A fire is built outside the lodge, usually to the East and the rocks which are to be carried into the lodge are placed on the fire in a cone shape. They are always of volcanic origin to ensure they withstand the heat and do not splinter. An altar is created out of earth to the east of the lodge and a spirit trail is laid connecting the fire to the altar and then to the fire pit which has been dug in the center of the lodge.

"The lodge chief traditionally enters the lodge to bless and awaken it with sage and cedar incense and sometimes with the sacred pipe, to pray and invoke the powers of the four directions. The people undress, line up on the left of the spirit trail and are smudged with sage and cedar incense before crawling into the lodge through the low doorway. The Sweatlodge is seen as the womb of Mother Earth and the ceremony is one of entering the darkness, dying to the old and coming out at the end cleansed of the past and reborn.

"Everyone sits round the central pit, close together in the small space. The rocks are brought in and blessed with sage. The first seven rocks

This page & opposite:
*The construction of a sweatlodge,
its fire-pit and the feeding fire.*

symbolize the four directions, the above and below and the Creator, Wakantanka, All-That-Is. Further stones are then brought in until the required temperature has been reached. The door is closed and the lodge chief calls in the powers, making an offering of water to the rocks at the end of each prayer. Usually, the first round of prayers is for oneself, since until one is in balance, anything one attempts to do for others will be tainted with one's own needs. The people pray one by one in turn in a clockwise circle and at the end of each prayer the chief puts another offering of water on the rocks, so the prayer is carried in the steam to the spirit world. At the end of the first round of prayers, the door is opened and drinking water is passed round.

"More red hot rocks will be brought in to introduce the second round of prayers, which are for anything and anybody except oneself. The same procedure continues and is followed by the third round, which is the round of the "give-away" prayer. Now one prays to let go of aspects of oneself that are ready for change and to offer one's gifts in service of spirit. The fourth round has no form; having prayed, it is time to listen. There

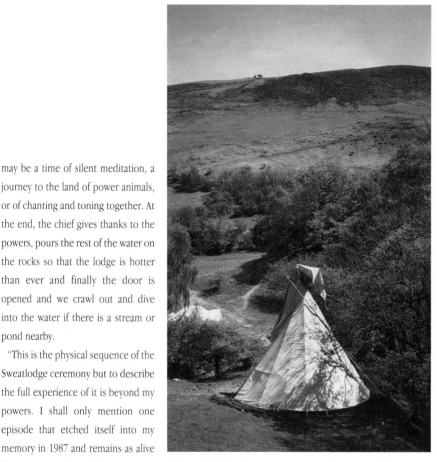

This page & opposite:
*The sweatlodge: the
apprentices' camp and
the ceremonial lodge.*

may be a time of silent meditation, a journey to the land of power animals, or of chanting and toning together. At the end, the chief gives thanks to the powers, pours the rest of the water on the rocks so that the lodge is hotter than ever and finally the door is opened and we crawl out and dive into the water if there is a stream or pond nearby.

"This is the physical sequence of the Sweatlodge ceremony but to describe the full experience of it is beyond my powers. I shall only mention one episode that etched itself into my memory in 1987 and remains as alive for me now as it was then. It was a special Deer Tribe healing sweat for apprentices and consisted of seven rounds instead of the usual four, with the door being opened once only. I was supposedly one of the more experienced "sweaters," so I was asked to sit next to the fire pit. As we were nearing the end, I experienced a moment when I could stand it no longer. Suddenly and uncontrollably I lost my center and burst forward out of the lodge and thankfully sprawled outside. After a while I began to wonder how I had got out so quickly; had I upset the bucket of water, had I damaged the structure in my hurry to get out and how much humble pie would I have to eat for losing

my space and making such a mess of things. Marius, one of the fire-people, looked after me as I lay on the ground and I remember watching people coming out of the lodge. I started asking what had happened but no-one would tell me—it felt very odd. Surely everyone must have seen me burst out like that, or at least have been disturbed by my precipitate action. No-one seemed to know anything! Finally, I got some sense out of Liz. She told me I was one of the last in the lodge and had to be nudged to come out at all."

I will let Stalking Wolf have the last word on Sweatlodges. He was the Apache Grandfather who taught Tom Brown immortalized in the books *The Vision*, *The Quest* and *The Journey*.

"You have felt the presence of the ancients, the expansion of self and the peace. You know now what a true ceremony should be, for as you felt the power of the lodge, so too will others, regardless of belief. The Sweatlodge speaks to all peoples in the language of their own beliefs and thus it becomes a universal truth. So, then, use the lodge as a tool, a doorway for physical and spiritual renewal and cleansing, a pathway to expansion and a vehicle to the worlds of the unseen and eternal."

KAHUNA RETREATS

THE KAHUNA ARE THE INDIGENOUS HEALER-SHAMANS OF THE Hawaiian islands. Dr. Serge Kahili King, the adopted grandson of a Kahuna from the island of Kauai, has brought the tradition into a Western context by running healing retreats on the island. His path, known as the "Way of the Adventurer," teaches practical ways of creating reality that are claimed to be as effective today as they were in the past. As a metaphor for this unbroken lineage of knowledge, he tells the following story:

"In the year 994CE a middle-aged man wearing a pure white robe made from the pounded bark of a tree squats down on an outcropping of lava rock, facing the ocean. From out of a woven raffia pouch he takes a worn stone carved to vaguely resemble a fish and sets it down on the black lava. In a trilling, chanting voice, he speaks to the stone, moving it in various directions in response to some internal impulse that only he is aware of. Finally, he stops chanting and smiles down at the piece of stone which now has its head towards

Right: *The spirit of aloha works unites the forces of Nature with the powers of the mind.*

Previous pages:
74. This house, built in the graveyard at Kalaupapa, once belonged to an Hawaiian Kahuna.

75. Ancient trees in a sacred Kahuna site on the island of Molokai, Hawaii.

the mountains behind him. He stands up and shouts to the fishermen who have been waiting.

"Prepare the nets. The fish will be here in abundance when the sun reaches Kahiki-Ku, in the late afternoon."

"In 1994 a young woman in a well-tailored business suit is on her way to an important meeting. In the window seat of the 747, she leafs through the airline magazine to pass the time. Suddenly, she puts the magazine down, aware of an event forming in her environment. Moments later, the plane shakes as it enters rough air, the seat belt lights go on and the captain announces that everyone should stay seated because of strong turbulence ahead. The woman takes a deep breath and extends her spirit beyond the confines of the airplane. She blends her energies with the wind, talks to it soothingly and smoothes it out with her mind. In two minutes the turbulence has gone. She lets go of her focus and returns to her reading."

The two people in the story, separated by a thousand years, are both adepts of the path of loving power; they know how to use the "spirit of aloha" to work in a loving way with the forces of Nature and the powers of the mind, for the benefit of social and environmental relationships and events. This is the broad purpose of Serge King's healing retreats. People come to Coconut Beach on Kuaui Island to receive the blessing of a beautiful environment and to learn techniques including the "hula kahiko," (the ancient sacred hula dance), telepathic healing and environmental healing with the art of geomancy. Like many Neo-shamans, King is a doctor of psychology and the author of a number of books.

THE WAY OF
THE HEART

CHRISTIANITY

RETREATS HAVE BECOME SO POPULAR AMONG CHRISTIANS IN the last decade or so that you normally have to book your room months in advance. Religious houses of every denomination continue the ancient practice of making rooms available for people who want to spend time on their own for reflection, or who want to revitalize their faith by joining a community's daily round of work and worship. The National Retreat Association in Britain acts as an information network for retreats of all denominations and there is a similar organization in the USA, called Retreats International. In an era like ours, which values subjective experience so highly, the traditional suspicion of the Church regarding personal mystical experience has had to give way to the mood of the times. Christianity has also had to compete with the influx of traditions from the East which are rich in practices of meditation and self-inquiry, as well as the self-questioning encouraged by psychotherapy. Having been protected for nearly two thousand years, Christianity is now having to respond to external challenges in a way it has never known before.

The low esteem in which Christianity has traditionally placed interior silence and contemplation is graphically illustrated by Thomas Merton's description in his autobiography, *Seven Storey Mountain*, of his life in a monastery, Gethsemani, in Kentucky.

Though the monastery is part of the Trappist Order, which has one

of the strictest of all monastic rules, including the rule of silence, Merton found that there was practically no time given for personal contemplation at all. The silence observed was external and internal silence was never alluded to. No methods or instruction in interior prayer were given and the day was filled with one activity or chore after another. The monks were as busy and preoccupied with running the farm and administering the monastery, as anyone in the daily world of business.

This criticism was shared by a woman I met recently at the Christian Meditation Center in London. Patrice is French and in 1980, when she was in her early twenties, she decided to enter a Trappist convent in Belgium; not because she was devoutly Christian but because she had a love of silence and wanted to live in a context where she could deepen her practice of interior contemplation. She stayed five years and left finally when she realized that the sisters and her elders simply did not have the language or the teaching to express contemplative experience. When she told the Abbess that she wanted to leave for

India, the Reverend Mother gave her a copy of the autobiography of Pere Le Seaux, a Benedictine monk who left his monastery for India in the fifties. "I understand you," she almost whispered, conspiratorially. "Take this but don't tell anyone I gave it to you."

The Church has been too at pains to uphold and preserve its external authority. Its own hierarchy is central to that authority and if individuals were free to have and believe in their own spiritual experiences, the power of bishops and priests would be seriously undermined. The low value attributed to contemplative prayer effectively barred Christians from the direct experience of God within themselves.

By the Renaissance, mystical experience had become not only suspect but verging on the unholy. With the rise of Protestantism, the Roman Church proclaimed it was necessary to "reconquer the world for Christ" with the result that outer action, rather than inner experience, came to be the dominant value of religious life. In the seventeenth century the spread of Quietism brought mysticism into even greater disrepute. Protestantism did little to right the balance, stressing ethics and morality alongside social action.

The Church maintained its revelatory authority to the exclusion of individual experience until the Second Vatican Council of 1964. Under the visionary guidance of Pope John Paul, the Council began dialogue with other faiths, sanctioning not only interfaith discussion but also personal explorations by inspired individuals within the monastic community itself.

The books and lectures of three men in particular brought the practices of Zen to the attention of the Christian public. Father William Johnston, Dom Aelred Graham and Thomas Merton all emphasized the need for reintroducing contemplative prayer and silence into the Christian life and discussed how the techniques and perspectives of Zen Buddhism could help this. All three pointed out the excess of

Right: *The gateway to the remote St. Anthony's Monastery, in the heart of the Egyptian desert.*

dogma and reliance on belief present in the Church; and suggested that there were lessons to be learned from Buddhism, "which seeks not to explain but to pay attention, to become aware... in other words to develop a certain kind of consciousness that is above and beyond deception by verbal formulas–or by emotional excitement." (Thomas Merton, *Zen and the Birds of Appetite*.)

Dom Aelred faces the core of the Christian dilemma in regard to contemplation. As long as Christ is conceived only as an historical person outside our own experience, who might intercede in our affairs if we call loudly enough, there is no framework to allow the existence of Christ living within our own hearts. He writes,

"In Mahayana Buddhism... the faithful are encouraged to believe that the Buddha's luminous state of consciousness, what is held to be his supreme degree of wisdom and compassion, is open to everyone. This is the prospect that is attracting so many in the West to Buddhism today–to which must be added its apparent harmony with much that is disclosed in the sciences of physics and psychology.

"To achieve the "mind of Christ" may well demand a profound re-thinking of Christianity's prayer life. Telling God, reverentially, what he should do and people, indirectly, how they ought to behave, together make up a good deal of the Church's vocal prayers. They are hardly enough for those who believe themselves to be sharers in the divine nature, who wish to realize experientially such a state and make it known to others." (Dom Aelred, *Contemplative Christianity*.)

In the late nineteen-fifties and -sixties, there were a few other individuals within the Church who were seeking to revitalize the practice of individual contemplation from within the ancient traditions of the early Church itself, rather than by referring to the practices of other religions. One of these was Carlos Carretto, a charismatic Italian who, as leader of the Catholic Action Movement, had been used to speaking to rallies of a million people or more in Saint Peter's Square. At the height of his career, he left everything to become a monk in the Sahara as one of the Little Brothers of the Desert, an order founded on the inspiration of

Charles de Foucauld. There Carretto came to the joyful realization that he was a man of no importance; the desert returned him to a sense of proportion. "Strip your prayers," he wrote in his *Letters from the Desert*; "simplify, de-intellectualize. Reach God not through understanding but love." Then, later: "If earlier we knew, we possessed something, now love has reduced us to nothing. Even the good thoughts serve no purpose now." Carretto could have been speaking for Zen, which points to what lies beyond thoughts altogether; he was following in the footsteps of the early Desert Fathers of the second and third centuries, when Christianity thrived as a living and vibrant tradition of interior prayer. The essence of that tradition was simplicity, a stripping away of all that lay between oneself and the mystery of God. After ten years in the Sahara, Carretto returned to Italy to found a retreat center near Assisi, on the southern slopes of Mount Subiaso. The community is patterned after the early Brothers of Saint Francis and runs week-long silent retreats throughout the year for ever-increasing numbers of lay people from all over Europe.

Right: *St. Simeon suggested that the mind "should guard the heart while it prays...."*

Left: *A hermit at rest in the porch of the monastery in Mount Athos.*

The early Desert Fathers continue to be the inspiration for the Orthodox Church which, unlike its Western counterpart, has never lost touch with its mystical roots. From the late sixties, the heart of Orthodox teachings on interior prayer, known as *The Philokalia*, began to reach a much wider audience than the Orthodox community itself. *The Philokalia*, a collection of writings from the desert fathers of the early church, attracted the interest of many people who wanted to practice interior prayer and who wanted to stay within a Western tradition rather than adopt practices from the East. One of the authors in *The Philokalia*, Saint Simeon the New Theologian, speaks of the "prayer of the heart," which has come to be the foundation of Orthodox practice: "the mind should be in the heart... it should guard the heart while it prays, revolve, remaining always within and thence, from the depths of the heart, offer up prayers to God... some of the fathers call this doing, silence of the heart; others call it attention..."

The mind is kept in the heart by the repetition of the "Jesus prayer": "Lord Jesus Christ, Son of God, have mercy on me, a sinner."

Sometimes, the prayer is reduced to a single interior cry of the Lord's name. It continues to be the main practice on Mount Athos, the peninsula in Greece which, with twenty-one monasteries on it, is still the center of Orthodox mysticism.

In the nineteen-seventies and -eighties, the Jesus Prayer was a precedent for two modern versions which have become widely used throughout North America. The first, the "centering prayer," was developed by Thomas Keating. Keating used to be the abbot of Saint Joseph's Abbey in Massachusetts but when his partiality to Eastern

Left: *One of the many monasteries built in extraordinary locations on Mount Athos, Greece.*

teachings and to interior contemplation became too much of an issue for his community, he moved to Snowmass Benedictine Monastery in Colorado, from where he continues to travel widely giving talks on the centering prayer and contemplation, which he sees as the union of knowledge and love. By knowledge he means gnosis, the Greek word in the bible that translates the original Hebrew word "da'ath"–"an intimate kind of knowledge involving the whole man, not just the mind." This higher, experiential knowledge comes through love–the love or striving that a man feels towards God and the love that God directs to man. The centering prayer helps to create the conditions that encourage this experience of gnosis. You take a prayer word or an image and keep your mind on it with a soft attention, thereby calming your mind and making it available to the deeper impulse of the true self. The centering prayer is now taught in Christian groups of all kinds throughout North America.

In the nineteen-fifties an English man, John Main, was introduced to meditation by an Indian monk while in the Foreign Service. Main later became a Benedictine monk and explored the writings of the desert fathers. In the works of John Cassian he discovered the theology of the indwelling spirit and the repetition of the prayer "Lord, Come," which in the original Aramaic was the word, "Maranatha." Paul used the Aramaic term in his letter to the Corinthians, who must have already known of it as a liturgical invocation in the celebration of the

Eucharist. The use of "Maranatha" in the liturgy was parallel to the use of the Hebrew "Amen" and "Alleluia." John Main recovered this simple tradition of silent prayer and began to use it as a modern version of the Jesus Prayer. He opened the Christian Meditation Center in London in 1975 to teach it to the lay public and in 1977 he went to Canada to found a small Benedictine community, where he died in 1982. There are now over one thousand groups in North America and Europe who organize regular retreats and meet weekly for the practice of "Christocentric" meditation. The purpose of the "mantra" is to leave all other thoughts, words and images behind in order to allow the pure prayer of Christ to well up in the depths of the individual being.

Of all the retreats now being run under the aegis of Christianity, these examples of contemporary contemplation still account for a minority. They represent the leading edge of Christian mysticism; most Christian retreats still include sermons, bible study and talking during meals and free time. Often people go to a Christian retreat simply to rest, or to take time away from the pressures of their habitual environment. In a culture as "doing" oriented as our own, a retreat can be immensely valuable on this count alone.

The scene is set for change; the established Church is facing a widespread grassroots movement which is recovering the early traditions of the Church for itself. The Church used to consist of a diverse network of local communities centered round an ardent prayer

Right: *Christian retreats have traditionally focused on prayer and bible study rather than solitary meditation.*

life, embracing varying points of view, encouraging the inner life of the individual. Contemporary conditions are encouraging such a Christian way of life again and the retreat movement is part of that revitalization process. In *Letters from the Desert* Carlos Carretto writes,

"The laity are becoming conscious of their mission and are searching for a genuine spirituality. It is truly the dawn of a new world to which it would not seem unworthy to give as an aim "contemplation in the streets" and to offer the means of achieving it."

One of the main distinctions between Christianity and the Eastern religions is the doctrine of grace, which affects one's entire attitude to the practice of prayer and the notion of retreat itself. A Buddhist retreat consists of a great deal of effort; even though Soto Zen speaks of "just sitting," a retreat means "just sitting" for thirteen hours a day, with a crack on the back as soon as your posture starts to slump. The idea is to break through your conditioning, including the common notion that meditation, like anything else, is something you "do." Arduous practice of this sort soon makes it quite clear how little you can do; how little you are in control of the mind. It drives you to give up your ordinary assumptions about yourself and the world, so that something else can make its presence known. To discover this, you have to make the effort in the first place.

Christianity assumes that there is little, if anything, that one can do to find God. God is simply beyond all our strategies. All that we can do is to make ourselves available; to have an inner disposition that is

Left: *The leaders of the Christian church are having to release some of their more traditional attitudes in order to embrace the spirit of contemporary Christianity.*

Opposite: *The traditional image of Catholicism: a woman prays to the Madonna in a chapel in Gibraltar.*

receptive to the grace of God. This is one of the roots of the notion of original sin—we are too opaque to know God but He in His grace can know us. Our task is to offer ourselves to Him, so that He may illuminate our darkened soul. This is the ideology behind the words of the Jesus prayer, which is meant to foster this attitude of availability.

Until recently, Christianity has assumed this capacity for availability to be a given of Church membership, whereas in truth most of us are not often open to anything beyond our own thoughts and feelings. Another word for this openness is that old Christian term, "repentance." The real meaning of this word has been obscured by negative associations; the original Greek term is "metanoia," which means literally "to

turn around," away from our own preoccupations and assumptions towards the unknown territory that is God. This is the purpose of the interior methods of prayer that have sprung up in the last twenty years–to foster that availability so that grace may be received.

The accent is on an atmosphere of grace, not the intensity of one's own effort. What effort there is, is of a subtle kind, a quality of surrender that does not require hours on a meditation cushion, allowing the grace of God to burst in on our lives at any moment. This underlying attitude is one of the main distinctions between a Christian retreat and a Buddhist one.

"As long as the soul is not still," writes Metropolitan Anthony, "there can be no vision. But when stillness has brought us into the presence of God, then another sort of silence, much more absolute, intervenes: the silence of a soul that is not only still and recollected but which is overawed in an act of worship by God's presence."

(Archbishop Anthony Bloom, *Living Prayer*.)

To be still, Bloom implies, requires a delicate effort of recollection, a gathering of one's intention and attention. The process is not as linear as it sounds and the distinction between effort and surrender is a subtle one. Both are required in any spiritual practice and it is how the emphasis is placed and the disposition of the individual practitioner which characterizes a particular path. Ramana Maharshi is considered one of the great sages of twentieth century India, a supreme embodiment of the path of wisdom. He recommended choosing between two distinct practices, according to one's nature: the way of rigorous self-inquiry, using the koan "Who Am I?;" or complete surrender of all responsibility for one's life to God. Ramana said that they both led to the same end and the latter is the Christian ideal.

Left and right: *The work of Hildegaarde of Bingen celebrates creation.*

Creation spirituality is a radical movement, aiming to replace the fall/redemption model of Christianity with a theology of creation and creativity that celebrates the qualities of Eros, pleasure, play and delight. It centers around the inspiration of Mathew Fox, a Dominican priest who was excommunicated for his views and activities. Fox is the director of the Institute in Culture and Creation Spirituality at Holy Names College, Oakland, California, which runs graduate programs in Creation Spirituality and every summer holds two-week-long retreats for people who want to make an introductory exploration into this recently revived form of Christianity.

Fox replaces the idea of original sin with original blessing (the title of one of his books). Humanity and the whole of creation is blessed perpetually by the presence of God and the natural response is joy and celebration. What deserves celebration is life itself in all its forms. This means an awareness of and response to nature; ecological necessities; and our inter-being with all other people. Creation-centered spirituality feels the deep pain of existence, yet remains passionate about the blessing that life is, communicating that passion through all forms of art and shared ritual.

Fox makes it clear that, far from being something he dreamed up in response to the tired theology of conventional Christianity, Creation

Spirituality is as old, if not older, than the fall/redemption model. It is to be found in the wisdom books of the bible, the psalms and in the works of the first Christian theologian in the West, S. Irenaeus (c. 130-200CE). Christ was creation-centered, as was Meister Eckhart, Hildegaarde of Bingen, Julian of Norwich, Nicholas of Cusa and many others. Instead of seeing suffering as the wages of sin, Creation Spirituality sees it as birth pangs of the individual and the universe. Death is a natural event, a prelude to rebirth; suspicion of the body is replaced by Eckhart's view that "the soul loves the body." Humility, instead of meaning "to despise oneself" (Tanquerry), means to befriend one's earthiness (humus).

These are the perspectives that are put forward at the summer retreats. Each day begins with a "body prayer," followed by a seminar, continuing in the afternoon with a variety of classes in Art as Meditation. These include "Mysticism through Sound, Singing and Music"; "Body as Sacred Source"; and "Native Spirituality and Ritual." The overall retreat aims to integrate a celebration of the wisdom of nature, native peoples and the Western mystical tradition with the scientific understanding of an emerging universe. The overall experience is intended to provide an holistic model for harmonious living that reflects reverence for all creation.

CHRISTIAN MEDITATION CENTERS

THESE GROUPS EXIST THROUGHOUT THE WORLD AND practice the Christian mantra meditation formulated by John Main. The various centers run periodic retreats to which all are welcome; the London center holds an annual summer retreat at the monastery of Monte Olivete, in Tuscany, Italy, while in Canada a retreat center has recently been established at Napanee, Ontario, half-way between Montreal and Toronto.

The retreatant is encouraged to let go of the "riches of thought and the imagination" and dwell on the mantra. The fruits of the practice are measured not in mystical experiences but in the degree of noticeable change in the way one goes about one's daily life. There are three levels of mantra meditation:

1. *Saying it—repeating it in the face of constant obstacles*
2. *Sounding it—repeating it without interruption*
3. *Listening to it—when it "says itself" without distraction*

The director of the London center, Laurence Freeman OSB, sees meditation as "the missing contemplative dimension of much Christian life today. It does not exclude other types of prayer and indeed deepens one's reverence for the sacraments and one's reading of scriptures."

Father Alphonse Timira writes of his retreat experience in *The Christian Meditation Newsletter*, 1993:

Opposite: *The Osage monastery,
Sand Springs, Oklahoma.*

"I can truly say I started meditating from the time I made Father Laurence's eight day retreat at the Franciscan Sister's Retreat Center at Maua in Moshi, Tanzania, in February 1982.

"When I arrived at the place for the retreat, I found gossip around that all the priest from Montreal talked about was the repetition of a word. Apparently, some people did not find much sense in talking about prayer as just repeating a word. In fact, a couple of days later, two of the retreatants discontinued the retreat, claiming it was a waste of their time. To everybody's surprise, the retreat master accepted their response with a smile. He proceeded calmly to suggest that the rest of us should feel free to do the same should we want. He then pointed out that sometimes it happens that people are not yet ready for that form of prayer.

"It sounded too simple to be true. In fact, when the retreat began and Father Laurence started talking about the use of the mantra as a way into silence–the silence of pure prayer–I did not quite grasp what it meant. It only came clear after we had meditated together in silence for thirty minutes. As Father Laurence stressed, it was of little use to talk about meditation without meditating. Lived experience here was the true teacher. Within a short time of making the retreat, I began to realize that this was what I had been unconsciously looking for over the years. It was like falling in love, albeit altogether different."

In the same newsletter, Father Laurence writes of his stay with Mother Teresa's contemplative sisters in Calcutta:

"Their house... is a simple but pristine oasis of peace in the middle of the slums and markets of this city which is forever defying the worst that a visitor could imagine. On one side of the community is the ancient graveyard of Saint John's catholic church, the final resting place of generations of Christian missionaries; on the other is Sealdah railway station, with its constant litany of platform announcements and the chants of the snack vendors.

"The sisters follow a disciplined but joyful and relaxed life of prayer, conscious of their spiritual presence at the heart of the daily lives of their active sisters who care for the poorest of the poor on the streets and in the hostels of the world each day. And because, as *The Cloud of Unknowing* said, no life is either completely active or completely contemplative, the contemplative Missionaries of Charity themselves spend two hours a day working and praying with the poor.

"Their life and situation teaches us, like so much else in India, by shocking us. One is not there long before thinking that their unlikely setting realizes the ideal of Christian contemplative living more fully than many an idyllic rural monastery that jealously protects its cloister from the world's contagion. Peace and silence in the midst of the dirt and chaos of such human turmoil confounds our expectations and assumptions (enlightenment happens, Zen teaches, when the road of thinking is blocked).

"When we visited Khaligat, the home for the dying where Mother Teresa began her missions of charity, I stopped beside the bed of an emaciated young man who had not spoken for days. In his eyes there was the penetrating look of pure compassion which was once, mercifully, caught for humanity in an unforgettable photograph of Ramana Maharshi.

"In such discomposing settings in India, more than in our cosseted and complaining western culture, one understands the value of meditation." Father Laurence's words echo those of Lama Yeshe, Retreat Master of Holy Island, who also points to compassion as being the ultimate motive for Tibetan meditation practice.

THE TAIZE COMMUNITY

*One passes through Taize
as one passes close to a spring of water.*

Pope John Paul XXIII

AIZE IS ONE OF THE MOST VIBRANT EXPRESSIONS OF Christian life to have emerged in the twentieth century and, like many great achievements, it began in a very small way. In 1940 Brother Roger, a Protestant, arrived in the small village of Taize, in Burgundy, France and remained alone there for two years, sheltering political refugees, mainly Jews. He was twenty-five years old. During that time he dreamed of starting a community that would span the different Christian denominations and serve as a living focus of reconciliation. He envisioned Taize to be the site of this new impulse.

Within a few years he had been joined by seven more brothers. In 1960, for the first time since the Reformation, Catholic bishops and Protestant pastors came together for three days at Taize. Pope John Paul XXIII invited Brother Roger for annual audiences and became an ardent supporter of the Taize initiative. From 1971 onwards there was a permanent representative of the Prior of Taize to the Holy See.

Taize began to attract increasing numbers of young people and by the late nineteen-seventies the community had become the symbol of Christian renewal for young people from all over the world. Today, as many as three thousand young people a year attend the weekly retreats, while church congregations elsewhere are almost entirely made up of the elderly.

What is it that young people find at Taize that they do not find in their church communities at home? Firstly, there is a spontaneous approach to life and worship that has drawn comparisons with the

Below: *Young people celebrate their faith at the Taize community.*

Right: *A retreatant's hut at Shantivanum, Tamil Nadu.*

Assisi of Saint Francis. The community shares with Francis a wariness of schematizing and creating unnecessary barriers. Then, there is a positive encouragement of celebration, of music, song, dance and community rituals. On Saturdays they hold the Festival of the Light of Christ, in which everyone enters the church with a lighted taper to celebrate the resurrection, and on Friday evenings, there is silent prayer around the cross, by which everyone present comes into communion with the suffering of the world.

The whole emphasis of Taize is on friendship and community: the sense of togetherness in spirit is tangible. Young people from all continents make up the majority of visitors and the sense of being part of an international community is truly inspiring. In the Church there is a copy of a seventeenth century Coptic icon from Egypt which shows Christ with his arm round the shoulder of a friend, walking alongside him. That friend, says Brother Roger, is each one of us. Brother Roger and the community see themselves as friends to all who visit, rather than as mentors. Their rôle is to listen.

Every year the brothers of Taize go to some of the poorest places on earth, not to give charity, or do anything in particular other than to express their solidarity with the underprivileged. They stay in the slums of Calcutta, on the edge of the Sahara, anywhere they can honor the humanity of those normally forgotten by the rich and powerful. Taize has always been careful to avoid any links with the power of money or politics. It accepts no gifts; the brothers do not even accept any family inheritance but live from their work alone. *The Letter from Taize* is published in nine languages every two months.

SHANTIVANAM

S HANTIVANAM IS A UNIQUE expression of Christianity in Ṭamil Nadu, southern India. It attracts people from all over the world who seek personal reflection and contemplation in an interfaith setting. It is an ashram which began to take on its present form in the 1950s when an English Benedictine monk, Father Bede Griffiths, came to India to found a Benedictine community and, as he put it, "to find the other half of his soul." As he came to know India and

something of the depth of its spiritual tradition, he came to realize that he was there as much to learn as to give.

What Hindu spirituality showed him above all was the need for interiority. Bede embarked on a serious study of classical Indian texts and of Advaita Vedanta, the non-dual tradition which characterizes the Upanishads. What he learned from his and the life of the villagers around him was to influence the whole direction of the ashram and of his personal spiritual journey. He saw that in India, everyday life was imbued with a sense of the sacred; that devotion and a sense of awe before the mystery of life were part of the Hindu's ordinary experience.

Shantivanam now serves the local community as a center for Hindu Christianity and the community of Sannyasins (renunciates) as a place of work and prayer. It is under the authority of the local bishop, affiliated to the Camaldoli Order, whose principal monastery is in Rome. The monks of Shantivanam go to Rome to join the Order then return and take the Hindu Sannyasin vow, renouncing all communal and brotherly ties for their solitary flight to God. In this way the Christian emphasis on community and the Hindu's concern for individual salvation are brought together.

The church at Shantivanam is indistinguishable from a Hindu temple, open on all sides, with carvings of the four evangelists looking like local gods. The services are a blend of Hindu chants and bible readings, communion and the Hindu fire ceremony, aarti. Guests join the community for meals, which are served in much the same way as in any monastery, with a daily reading continuing as people eat in silence. Retreatants stay in little huts, while other guests stay in double rooms or dormitories. Silence is maintained in the afternoon. Father Bede died in 1993 but two Indian monks, Brothers Martin and Christadas, run the ashram with the same inspiration and are available for spiritual direction.

A Shantivanam retreat is many things: the stillness and peace of rural India, with the soft waters of the sacred river Cauvery flowing by; Bede's legacy of cross-cultural spirituality; the rhythm of shared worship and solitary reflection; and the stimulation of a small but multi-national gathering of like-minded people. Your stay should be arranged in advance by writing to the ashram. Payment is by donation.

Below (left): *Prayer at the Osage monastery.*

Below (right): *The Osage monastery, Sand Springs.*

Left: *Life at Shantivanum: afternoon tea, waiting for lunch, eating under a portrait of Bede Griffiths.*

OSAGE

The Osage ashram in Oklahoma runs on similar principles to Shantivanam. The founder, Senor Pascalene, was inspired by Bede's vision of universal spirituality within a Christian setting. Osage is available for individual and small group retreats. It also runs its own program.

SUFISM

A lover may hanker after this or that love,
But at the last he is drawn to the King of love.
However much we describe and explain love,
When we fall in love we are ashamed of our words.
Explanation by the tongue makes most things clear,
But love unexplained is clearer.

(Jalal'ud-din Rumi, *The Spiritual Couplets.*)

Sufism is the mystical branch of Islam. One explanation for the term is that it derives from a word meaning wool and refers to the rough cloth worn by the mystics of the early Middle Ages; another is that the word comes from the Arabic, "safa," meaning purity. Traditional Sufism remains among the most secretive and elusive of all contemporary spiritual paths. Your first difficult task with the Sufis will be to find them in the first place. If you do manage to find a traditional group, it will not be through reading an advertisement. You may need to convert to Islam, for Sufism normally remains embedded in the cultural framework from which it stems. The Sheikh will always be a male, as will the majority of the disciples.

Left: *A modern meditator in Morocco wears a wonderfully embroidered woolen coat, reminiscent of the rough wool cloaks worn by mystics in years gone by, who were perhaps the ancestors of today's Sufis.*

Below: *The Sufi order of the Mevlevi focus their prayer on Sema, the sacred dance in which the dancer spins around the still center of his own heart.*

The essence of the Sufi path is known as the alchemy of the heart, a process which both requires and enables action, love and knowledge. Human perfection (enlightenment) is considered attainable through a gradual purification of the personality which enables the lower soul nature to be infused and led by the higher. The word "Islam" itself means submission, or surrender, so Sufism is in fact the true practice of Islam, requiring submission to Allah; for this the heart needs to be "polished like a mirror" so that it can reveal the presence of God which is its essence. An old Sufi tradition says: "Neither My Earth nor My Heaven can contain Me; but the Heart of My believing Servant contains Me." One of the most common Sufi practices for the polishing of the heart is the "dhikr," the repetitive chanting of God's name. This is not only an interior practice, as it is for the Orthodox Christians with their Jesus Prayer but a collective one, usually performed with great vigor by the dervishes in the presence of their Sheikh. The point of the "dhikr Allah" is to turn the devotee's attention away from himself to the remembrance of God. There are three stages in the performance of the dhikr: first you try to do it; then you do do it; then it does you. This leads to the ultimate spiritual state of the "self-having-passed-away-in-God," known as "fana," when the Sufi realizes existentially the truth of Divine Unity. This is the underlying aim of all Sufi practices.

Sufism is divided into a number of different schools, each of them centered around the presence of a Shaikh, who embodies the teaching of the school's lineage. The lineage is transmitted from Shaikh to Shaikh and often stretches back to a particular saint of the Middle Ages, though ultimately it begins with Mohammed Himself. The relationship between Shaikh and disciple is of central importance in the process of purification, for the practice of submission to the Master is a reflection of one's willingness to submit to God. Different Shaikhs will give different practices, depending on their school and personal inclination. Recitations of prayers and dhikrs are sometimes made with movement or dance, like the whirling Mevlevi Dervishes. Chants are often done to synchronized breathing patterns, which involve the body as well as the mind and heart in the prayer. Individual retreats are part of a disciple's practice and the nature and duration of the retreat—usually three days, a week, or forty days—is determined by the Shaikh. A description of a

Left: Rumi, the founder of the Mevlevi school, pictured here outside a blacksmith's shop.

forty-day Sufi retreat is given in the section Solitary Retreats. Perhaps the best known Sufi Order in the Western world is the Mevlevi, whose members are known through their performances of the Sema, the sacred dance in which the dancer spins around the still point of his own heart, with one hand outstretched towards heaven to receive blessings and the other turned towards the earth to transmit them.

The founder of the school was Jalal'ud-Din Rumi, the great Sufi saint of the thirteenth century. Rumi was already a Master and a renowned scholar in his own right when he met Shams of Tabriz in 1244. Their first meeting was when Shams burst into Rumi's study and threw his books out of the window, saying that love had no need of them. Shams awakened Rumi to the ultimate spiritual surrender but Rumi's disciples were jealous of their Master's relationship with the unlearned and unruly Shams; they conspired to kill the one who had stolen their Master's affections. Sham's murder prompted Rumi to pour out some

of the most ardent and inspired spiritual love poetry the world has ever seen. He wrote, "The time has come for me to dance in a circle; with face unveiled, Love is singing love-poems." Eight hundred years later, there are branches of the Mevlevi all over Turkey (where Rumi lived), the United States and Europe.

Some Western teachers who have been exposed to traditional Sufi teachings in the Near and Middle East have begun schools in the West that are more adapted to Western culture and mentality; here, the cultural trappings of Islam are usually absent; women and men are treated equally and there is no need to embrace Islam. The first of these teachers was George Ivanovitch Gurdjieff, who taught in Paris and New York in the nineteen-thirties and -forties. A more recent example is Oscar Ichazo, who founded the Arica School in the nineteen-seventies. Today, the most widely known teacher of Westernized Sufism is Pir Vilayat Khan, head of The Sufi Order of the West.

THE SUFI ORDER OF THE WEST

THE SUFI ORDER OF THE WEST WAS FOUNDED BY HAZRAT Inayat Khan, whose son, Pir Vilayat Khan, is the current head of the Order. Hazrat came from a well-known family of musicians in Baroda, India and was one of India's leading players of the vina at the beginning of the twentieth century. He was also a member of the Sufi Christi Order, which is still one of the most influential Sufi groups in the sub-continent today. Hazrat's teacher dreamed that the boy would be the first person to bring Sufism to the West; that dream became a reality. Hazrat came to the West in 1910 with his two brothers and they became celebrated musicians. Hazrat married the niece of Mary Baker Eddy, the founder of Christian Science and settled in London and Paris. They had four children and Hazrat began a Sufi school called The Sufi Order of the West.

Hazrat died in 1927 and passes the succession of The Sufi Order of the West to his son, Pir Vilayat Khan, who was just eleven years old. He went to the Sorbonne and earned a degree in psychology, spending time at Oxford. In the war he saw active service in the English submarine fleet, while his sister was the famous Madeleine, the French Resistance fighter who was the last radio operator behind enemy lines. She was betrayed, and was tortured and murdered by the Nazis. By the seventies Pir was widely known throughout the United States and Europe for his ecumenical brand of teaching.

The Sufi Order of which he is head has taken Sufi teachings and related them to other Wisdom traditions, forming a synthesis which might aptly be described as a perennial wisdom to be found under different names all over the globe. Individual, small group and large group retreats form a central part of the teaching of The Sufi Order of the West, and are available at a number of centers in North America and Europe. The Order's Retreatants undergo extensive training before being given permission to teach. Many of them are also counselors, psychologists and psychiatrists by profession.

The purpose of the retreat is to leave the world behind and discover a deeper self, which recognizes its inter-connectedness with all dimensions of being. The retreatant discovers qualities which are not easily perceived in daily life, and begins to view ordinary life and problems from a fresh vantage point. The retreats, which last from three to seven days, are designed to integrate this new awareness of oneself into a renewed vision of identity and life purpose.

Various methods and meditation techniques are taught by the Retreat Guide, especially the use of sound and music. The Guide may also introduce attunements from different spiritual traditions. The diet will be vegan and the retreat will take place in silence.

The Sufi Order of the West describes the transformation encouraged by their retreats in alchemical terms. The first half, consisting of three stages, is the "solve," or the dissolving period, the "dark night of the soul" described by Saint John of the Cross. Psychologically, it is a recognition and consequent breaking down of the self-image, the ego structure that builds up over time. The second half of the process, also consisting of three stages, is the "coagule." Central to this is the reconstitution of the person around a spiritual core.

"All this is words, though," says Sarida Brown, a Retreat Guide living and working in Britain. "It is the experience of a retreat which is life-giving: the freedom of flying on the wings of one's soul, finding the sacredness at the source of being, glimpsing who one really is and participating in the reality beyond individuality. These experiences change people deeply and generate the power to be creative of themselves and of life. I remember the ecstasy, on my first retreat in 1978, of discovering the silent language of the soul."

BHAKTI YOGA

Bhakti Yoga is generally understood as the way of devotion and surrender. In India it is often an integral part of other paths, such as Raja Yoga, as well as being a way of its own.

Few words have been more frequently misinterpreted, not only by Westerners but also by Eastern teachers, as "devotion" and "surrender." In Christianity, the interpretation is the surrender of the personal will to the will of God. In Hindu spirituality, the meaning is essentially the same except Christ is usually replaced by the guru, who may or may not be alive. If the guru is dead, then the dynamic between disciple and guru is often not dissimilar to that between Christian and Christ. If the guru is alive, however, the psychology of the individuals–both guru and disciple–can make the matter more complicated.

The fact that we in the West have been conditioned to think of surrender in absolute terms–the dissolution of personal will into the divine–without any real knowledge of what is meant or where we are starting out from, is one of the reasons so many people think the notion is not only absurd but also downright unhealthy. To surrender a personal identity that we have spent so long creating seems nothing less than an act of destruction. The misconception that surrender is something the ego can decide to do is what motivates the emotional posturing that so often surrounds a contemporary guru; the ego imitates, quite sincerely, the attitudes and emotions that it imagines it is meant to be experiencing.

Traditional Bhakti Yoga starts in the beginning. Most of us are in a relatively closed emotional state. We experience anger, fear, jealousy,

Below: *The spiritual master Osho still attracts devotion and love today, even though he left the physical body in 1990.*

Opposite: *Ram Dass and friend*.

sadness, easily enough but we are all too often opaque to our more subtle feelings; our inter-being with others, a sense of belonging and more deeply, the realization that we are loved by God. This is the essence of Bhakti Yoga–not emotion but the intense experience of love. Jacob Needleman, in an interview with Metropolitan Anthony, remarked how struck he had been by the absence of emotion in the voices of the singers of the liturgy in the Russian Orthodox church.

"Yes," Metropolitan Anthony replied, "that is quite true. It has taken years for that but they are finally beginning to understand... We have to get rid of emotions... in order to reach... feeling.... The proper response to love is to accept it. There is nothing to do. The response to a gift is to accept it. Why would you wish to do anything?" (Jacob Needleman, *Lost Christianity*.)

The chants and the music that accompany Bhakti Yoga have this as their purpose: the awakening of the deeper feeling level of our being, so that we may experience the fact that we are loved. The presence of the guru is an embodiment of that love which is available to all, whether it is recognized or not. Bhakti tends to bypass the mind and work directly on that part of our nature which is usually the most constricted–the heart. Once the heart is open, we do not stop thinking: we move our thinking to the heart so everything else can fall into place. Our heart reveals itself through openness and compassionate awareness and above all, the emanation of love.

From this perspective, surrender arises naturally out of the awareness of the deep heart. The normal condition of the ego, with its anxious sense of control, is relinquished not so much by effort but by a falling away. What emerges in its place is a disposition of surrender to "life as it is." When Needleman saw Metropolitan Anthony for the first time in some years, he noted that "there is something in his face now that I had not seen before... hard to put into words... a quality of openness that one might wish to describe as "surrender," a surrender not to any individual–or to any particular force one could name. In fact, there was something impersonal about it."

This is the surrender that a guru with the stature of a Sai Baba or an Ammaji can engender. By holding their image in mind or by chanting their name, one is bringing the attention of the heart round to receive that impersonal love of which they are a living expression. As one's openness expands, so does the faith in the guru and in one's own capacity to love. They will not ask you to believe anything, nor to make dramatic oaths of allegiance or discipleship. They will not try and hold on to you. Their grace is there; whether you avail yourself of it or not is up to you. This is the method of guru, or Bhakti Yoga.

To take a Bhakti Yoga retreat is not to commit yourself to a movement or a teacher: it is to place yourself in a context which will encourage a deeper openness and awakening of feeling, primarily through chanting, music and talks. If you continue to go to the same retreats, then it will be because you are entering naturally into a deeper relationship with the teacher and the teaching. No-one will ever ask you to surrender your discernment or your gut feelings.

RAM DASS RETREATS

"DO YOU KNOW THE STORY OF MY FATHER GIVING ME THE railroad business to run when I was hardly twenty five?" We were eating chicken fried rice somewhere in Boston in 1986. Yes, I did have a vague memory of some such story but the details escaped me. Ram Dass proceeded to fill me in. That lunch lasted three hours. We had to be gently nudged by the waiter to realize they were waiting to close.

Why might I have known the railroad story? Or any other of the stories I heard that day? The question came to me only later and the answer was simple. Ram Dass is perhaps the major living public representative of the Western seeker. His life has become a legend in America and to some extent in Europe as well. His outer life and its various dramas have almost become public property. He recounts the stories as if they belong more to the listener than to himself, with an amused detachment cultivated, I suspect, by years of extricating himself from the popular confusion of identity, between actor and role.

The legend began in the heady days of the 1960s when, as Richard Alpert, a Harvard psychology professor in league with Timothy Leary, he was sacked for turning his students on to LSD. Then came India, the meeting with his guru, Neem Karoli Baba, and the publication of *Be Here Now*, a landmark of its time. Neem Karoli died in 1973 and throughout the decade Ram Dass, as Neem Karoli named him, plunged into an all-consuming study and practice of Buddhist meditations, Tibetan tantric teachings and yogic disciplines. He was responsible for

Left & Opposite:
*Ram Dass encourages
warmth and connection
between people at all
levels of life. He is one
of the most accessible
spiritual teachers in
the West today.*

bringing Muktananda to the West and helped Chogyam Trungpa found the Naropa Institute of Buddhist Studies in Boulder, Colorado.

So what was the railroad story? It was really about Ram Dass's early relationship with power and authority in relation to others. He has always attracted positions of power and has usually found himself side-stepping them.

Though he has a huge following, he has consistently avoided having a center or a formal group of students. When Neem Karoli died, some of his followers looked to Ram Dass to take up the succession, as a kind of Head Boy; a proposal that Ram Dass managed to diffuse by referring to the authority of his guru, who had told him that rather than being a formal teacher, Ram Dass should commit himself to a life of service in the more general sense.

This is what he has done. His main work now is acting as fund-raiser for the Seva Foundation, an international relief agency. He runs retreats for the general public throughout the United States and in the UK, some of which are part of his fund-raising effort. All aim to introduce people to spiritual life in an accessible, cross-cultural way.

Ram Dass never presents himself as a guru, rather as a friend or brother who is traveling the same way as the retreatants; one who has

made the same mistakes that they have and is still learning as he goes. He uses a variety of methods from different traditions but the general tone of a Ram Dass retreat is one of expanded feeling and devotion towards God in all his various forms. Ram Dass himself is essentially a Bhakta and this is what characterizes his own relationship with his guru, and the overall atmosphere of the retreat but in a soft, undemonstrative way that allows people's hearts to open without any particular effort having to be made.

There are chanting sessions morning and evening and several periods of Buddhist Vipassana meditation daily, but most of the time is given to Ram Dass telling his stories and discussing themes of particular interest to those present. His great gift is to make Hindu and Buddhist teachings accessible to the Western mind, with a sense of humor that has people laughing daily. Meals are usually in silence, as are other designated periods of the day. Ram Dass calls his retreats "mature ashrams," allowing individuals to decide for themselves just how much of the schedule they want to attend. In practice, everyone attends everything but the choice is always there to skip something if you need some time on your own. The major New Age Retreat Centers in the last section of this book all host Ram Dass retreats.

MATA AMRITANANDAMAYI ASHRAM

AMRITANANDAMAYI, OR AMMA, IS IN THE LINEAGE OF THE ecstatic, devotional saints of southern India. She was born in 1953 to poor fisherfolk. When she was five she began composing songs to Krishna, for whom she had felt devotion the moment she heard of him. At nine she had to abandon school to care for her ailing mother, do all the domestic chores and tend the animals. The hostility and indifference of her family made her seek refuge in Krishna, whom she began to see regularly in visions. By seventeen, she knew the experience where all is perceived as the same divine essence. She began to reject food, sleep and shelter and spent day

and night meditating on the Divine Mother. Remaining for months in a state of bliss, one day she heard a voice within:

"My child, I dwell in the heart of all beings and have no fixed abode. Your birth is not merely for enjoying the Bliss of the Self but for comforting humanity. Henceforth worship me in the hearts of all beings and relieve them of the sufferings of their worldly existence."

From that day on, Amma has dedicated her life to sharing her love and grace with others. Her ministry is based on simplicity and love and although she has had no formal instruction, she uses the language of Vedanta, the philosophy of the non-dual, to convey her message.

Right & opposite: *Amma reaches people world-wide through her teachings and ecstatic singing.*

Rather than give discourses or formal instruction she teaches through her presence and her ecstatic singing to God. To see her sing is an electrifying experience; she appears to call down heavenly powers and lift her audience to the divine. All who come to her are embraced personally, as if a mother were re-uniting with a long-lost son or daughter. The concept of God as Divine Mother is central to her teaching. Speaking in Moscow in 1993, Amma said,

"I am not just a Hindu woman coming to Russia trying to convert you to another religion. I come in a difficult moment of Russian history to give people hope for the future. In the past... Russia was ruled by the masculine and now it is time to be influenced by the feminine. We do not know each other's language and yet we are like two banks of the same river. On the bottom of the river is God's love that unites us. Mother hopes that her love will unite us who seem so independent of each other."

This feminine influence is central to Amma's work: she is a living example of how the masculine emphasis in religion can be balanced. Nothing is demanded in return—you do not have to belong to anything, give anything, or commit yourself to anybody. Amma simply encourages you to re-establish your own connection with the essential part of yourself, affirming the perennial truth of all religions, "the kingdom of God is within you."

Amma travels round the world every year but is based in her ashram in Kerala, southern India. Other ashrams exist in California and in France. In 1993 she spoke as the Hindu representative at the parliament of the World's religions in Chicago. Always emphasizing the necessity of helping the poor and needy, Amma has set up educational, medical and employment programs all over southern India and has responsibility for an orphanage of four hundred children. She is active in the running of her own ashram and is often to be seen in the midst of some work project there, alongside everyone else.

There are around one hundred resident disciples at the ashram in Kerala and hundreds more at any one time as guest retreatants. Guests are free to take part in the daily schedule according to their wishes. The day begins at 5.00AM with the chanting of the one thousand names of the Divine Mother, meditation and then yoga. There are three more meditation session during the day and another session of devotional singing. The traditional ashram rules of celibacy, quiet speech and modest dress are observed. Amma gives a daily darshan (audience) for visitors, who are expected to contribute a minimum of one hour's work a day to the ashram.

THE WAY OF
THE BODY

God guard me from those thoughts men think
In the mind alone; He that sings a lasting song
Thinks in a marrow bone.

W. B. Yeats

ONE OF THE MOST SIGNIFICANT DEVELOPMENTS IN psychology and therapeutic technique over the last two decades has been the recognition of bodily experience as an indicator of a person's well-being. Having inherited a spiritual tradition which has devalued the body for two millennia, it is hardly surprising that some approaches have swung in the opposite direction and have bypassed the mind and rational thinking in the name of greater body awareness.

Most techniques and practices available now emphasize the interrelationship between body and mind. To minimize the value of the mind is as unproductive as denying the body, especially since we have spent ten thousand years developing the faculty of rational thinking. Even so, it is true that in the West, we are only just beginning to remember that the body has its own intelligence. In earlier eras and in other parts of the globe, the intelligence of the body was held in high regard. Yoga and Tai Chi are just two of the better-known paths to wholeness which Oriental traditions have developed to awaken the body's wisdom.

To go on a retreat of any kind will involve the body intelligence in some way. Shamanism and ritual practices get us to "walk our talk": to express our feelings and attitudes in bodily movement. Even a personal retreat without any particular form or discipline gives the body a chance to speak. In a context of silence and rest, the body will naturally start to release its tensions and allow its deeper needs and intuitions to come to the surface.

Right: *Certain physical disciplines can open up the flow of spiritual energy within the practitioner.*

Previous pages:
114. The practice of yoga will silence and center one's body.

115. When given silence and rest, one's body will begin to express its deeper needs.

Meditation in all its different forms requires a certain attitude that is reflected in posture. Rather than the common condition of feeling like a taut string on the one hand or a slack one on the other, meditation encourages a movement and flow which gives a sense of being properly tuned. The point is to be relaxed but alive, more receptive to states of being and feeling that a tenser or slacker body would be opaque to. In meditation, the interplay between body and mind becomes more tangible. The body will subtly shift according to the degree of openness and availability in the mind of the person and, as the body opens, so does the mind. The chin drops forward a little; the head resumes its natural balance on the top of the spine; the spine lengthens, the shoulders drop, the chest widens. Each tiny shift in the body is a reflection of falling deeper into silence.

The temptation is to try to set it all up to begin with. Many meditation teachers adjust the posture of their pupils and, while this external assistance may help the practitioner to become aware of his actual, rather than imagined, state, there is no "right posture" for openness, availability and attention. There are guidelines that need to be followed: it is not easy to be open when slumped in a chair, arms and legs crossed. What needs to be done is more than any mechanical manipulation. One has to start with a recognition of one's tension or

slackness and be open to being moved, literally, from within. When we learn to truly gather our attention, we discover for ourselves that certain postures and gestures—often taught in yogas and contemporary therapeutic techniques—are spontaneous physical manifestations of inner states of being. This is what Jacob Needleman reported in his book, *Lost Christianity*:

"I asked Metropolitan Anthony again about the work with the body, about the methods, the exercises I knew were in the Christian tradition—somewhere, in some time. Where did they come from? Where have they gone? I waited for him to continue. He said something about the Athonite Christians having this work with the body and then paused once again. Finally, he raised his eyebrows towards me. "You have been to our service. If you stand in the service with your hands down to the side, with your head slightly down—not too much—your weight evenly balanced... if one does this, one begins to see changes taking place in the body. The breathing changes, certain muscles relax, others become firm, not tense. All this comes from the religious impulse..." Again a pause. He continued, speaking softly and deliberately. "The exercises you ask about originated in this way: from the Fathers observing what happened to them when they were in a state of prayer."

Left: *At the Kripalu center, retreatants work with their own physicality to increase their spiritual growth.*

The purpose of the great systems of spiritual body training is to evoke the religious/spiritual impulse through work on the body. All of these systems have certain attitudes in common. The first is that the body, far from being a solid mechanical apparatus, is a dynamic system which is sustained by a flowing body of energy. In working with posture, the direction of sensation, different movement patterns and with the breath, they aim to awaken this energy and to encourage its flow through the various vital centers. This energy is the "chi" of Tai Chi, the "prana" of yoga. In Hindu mythology, this energy is the life-force of the universe and it is still venerated through the image of the Divine Mother, the first image to be worshipped by mankind all over the world. The spiritual intelligence that sustains the whole of creation is the same energy which lives in and through individual bodily existence. It is the "breath inside the breath" of every being and, on the universal scale, is the Dharma or, for the ancient Chinese, the Tao.

"The Tao is the breath that never dies. It is a Mother to All Creation. It is the root and ground of every soul–the fountain of Heaven and Earth, laid open." (Man-Ho Kwok, *Tao Te Ching*.)

Below: *When one is in balance physically, states of deep feeling can be invoked.*

In Plato's philosophy of the Great Chain of Being, which has a parallel in every other ancient civilization, humanity occupies a position on the scale of evolution mid-way between the angelic and the animal worlds. The individual's spiritual task is to serve as a bridge between these realms and to place the lower in himself at the service of the higher. The body is the immediate indication of how far this work has progressed. It is also the vehicle for establishing the bridge between the two worlds. All the martial arts, yoga, Tai Chi and other traditional body practices seek to do this in the first instance by establishing the individual's center of gravity in the middle region of the body, known to the Japanese as "hara."

Many of us walk in the world energetically out of balance. Our consciousness is directed too heavily towards the upper realm or the lower. In the former case, the figure appears to strain upwards negating its vital relationship to the earth. Such a person walks, stands or sits with their body taut like a string. They do not tread firmly but bob up and down, as if denying their natural weight. The center of gravity is lifted into the upper chest, inflating it with self-importance, anxiety and reactivity. The protruding chest and the arched back that supports it together attempt to sustain a picture to the world of someone who can win through. Considerable tension is needed to hold oneself and one's world up in this way.

What motivates this tension is the fear of its opposite: collapse. The hypertension of the typical Westerner is sporadically punctuated with periods of exhaustion and illness. There is the sensation of lack-luster, lifelessness, the center of gravity drops through the floor and the person barely feels capable of shouldering anything.

What body practices do is to shift the center of gravity away from the extremities to the area just below the navel. One learns to feel oneself permanently down there and to support the upright posture from the lower rather than from the upper back. A person who lives from "hara" will find that their whole person becomes less rigid. They begin to realize that the power flowing into them from below is not the product of their own will but that it comes from somewhere else; that they have only to let it in and guard it. They become aware of power within them which was previously blocked by an unbalanced posture, the physical expression of an ungrounded ego.

The other common element in bodywork is that the body is closer to the feeling sensibility than the mind is. All spiritual traditions emphasize the importance of accessing the feeling nature and its qualities of openness and availability. One can talk knowledgeably about openness all day, without feeling open at all; the conscious ego, which is based primarily in the rational mind, can convince itself that it is open even when it is blatantly obvious to everyone else that it is closed. The intelligence of the body, however, is not deceived in the same way. Body and feeling have a more direct, intimate connection with each other than the mind has with either and they quickly reveal each other's true condition. Many of the Sufi body exercises, including the whirling of the Mevlevi Dervishes, are designed to evoke deep states of feeling, ordinarily inaccessible.

The body is our contact with universal forces. Just as important, it is our contact with the present moment. Wherever our thinking may take us, our body is always right here, just where we are. To return to the body is to return to our own presence. By taking a retreat, we allow the body to return us to ourselves naturally; body practices help make that return more conscious, and root us more deeply in both the elemental and the spiritual worlds.

TAI CHI

THERE ARE MANY TAI CHI SCHOOLS throughout the USA and Europe, each with their particular approaches and methods. Probably the most artistic and creative exponent of the form in the West today is Chungliang Al Huang, founder of The Living Tao Foundation. Al Huang grew up in China where he received training in the classics, a variety of Oriental fine arts and martial arts. As well as heading the Living Tao Foundation, he is the director of the Lan Ting Institute, a cross-cultural study and conference center based at the historic Wu Yi Mountain in the People's Republic of China. His favorite way of describing the origins of Tai Chi is with the following story.

"Once upon a time, somewhere, anywhere in the world, there was a man (or a woman) sitting on a mountain top, quietly observing nature. He became so inspired by the movements of the world around him that he began to dance, imitating all the natural elements he could easily identify. He opened himself completely to the forces of nature. He became the forces: sky, earth, fire, water, trees, flowers, wind, cloud, birds, fishes butterflies. His dance became ecstatic, completely transforming and transcendent. So happy with himself, he then poetically named each movement motif: Bubble of the Cosmos, Yin/Yang Harmonic Loop, White Cranes Flashing Wings, Cloud-Waving Hands, Golden Birds Balancing on One Leg, Embrace Tiger Return to Mountain.

"He or she was the originator of the Tai Chi dance. This moment of creation could have happened thousands of years ago, or could have

happened right now. This moment could be somewhere, anywhere, in the world. This person could be you."

Tai Chi is the artless art of moving meditation. It goes back to the first moment a man felt a sense of himself and a need to orient himself in his environment, to find balance and harmony in a shifting, uncertain world. In the unrecorded past of China, there were people who realized that to find this balance, they needed to return to the original material of their being, pu, before it was trimmed and modified by experience. Pu is the basic substance of the self, one's raw essence. Tai Chi is a way of effecting a return to this natural state, of allowing the pu to emerge.

Al Huang has said that the first Tai Chi masters created the form out of the enlightenment of their own nature, awareness of their own body and their identification with nature. At its best, it flows so naturally it looks like you just made it up on the spot but it takes years of practice to reach this level.

Tai Chi begins with a sense of awareness and being and all movement patterns stem from there. You discover the variations of movement; you allow the circular flow to take you in different directions and bring you back almost to the original spot where you began. Tai Chi is neither a set structure nor chaos; the body movement is the motion of the universal order that the Chinese call the Tao.

To practice Tai Chi is to allow the body to move easily and unselfconsciously.

"Move, let move, be in touch with the movement within us, already moving. Follow the initiatives of least resistance. Avoid temptations to

Right & left: *Tai Chi brings strength and awareness into life, regardless of age or nationality.*

Previous pages:
122. An ancient Chinese bronze medallion, inscribed with the Tai Chi symbol surrounded by the eight hexagrams of the I Ching.

123. Early morning Tai Chi practice in a Hong Kong park.

manipulate the inevitable motion. Experience the sequential waves connecting place to place within our bodies. Feel the energy circulating from the soles of the feet to the crown of the head, from fingertips to toes. Be aware of the crossing point in the middle of the body that we call "dantien"–the focus of our life force. Allow the dantien to maintain for us this balance and equilibrium. Do not fight the tendency of imbalance. Enjoy the dynamics of not holding fast to the static center. Recognize that harmony can only be meaningful through the union of differences in their alternate changing process. Unity is a dance of multi-dimensional loops of interweaving forces." Al Huang and his staff run a large program of Tai Chi retreats and trainings across the United States.

THE SCHOOL OF TAI CHI CHUAN

THIS SCHOOL RUNS PROGRAMS THROUGHOUT THE USA AND IN many parts of Europe from its headquarters in New York City. The school was founded by Professor Patrick Watson. In 1966 Watson, already an accomplished martial artist, became the devoted disciple of Professor Cheng Man Ch'ing, the last seated Grand Master of Martial Art. After years of study and practice, Cheng gave Watson the task of developing a Western style for the teaching of Tai Chi. The school has since taught thousands of students and trained almost two hundred instructors. Margaret Olmsted wrote in the *Tai Chi Press* the following recollection of her last meeting with Watson, who died in 1992.

"A few weeks before Patrick died I went to visit him in New York. He lay on his bed, very thin and pale but peaceful. He asked me what we were working on in Push Hands class and I tried to explain it to him. He shook his head and sat up on the edge of the bed and had me stand in a 70/30 position in front of him. He put a frail hand on me and immediately I lost my balance. He said I was being too external with the new material I was learning and that I had to go more inside. I tried again but was completely unable to remain in principle as this old man followed and thwarted my efforts to remain in balance. He said to keep practicing."

One student wrote the following in his journal on a Tai Chi retreat at the New York School:

"We are about to start the Form again... sink, be aware of the point of balance in the lower belly and the vitality that concentrates there. The movement unfolds but I'm thinking too much, struggling with it... remember the strength of softness... feet rooted deep, a weight of a thousand tons hanging from the spine's base and the crown of the head upright on a thread from the center of the universe... too many words.

"Everyone is in the Form now, we are like one moving, living thing, one life and one consciousness of life... the words stop and my body is sheathed in a delicate well-being and the motion becomes effortless, the body moving itself. Such a simple thing.

"Later we do Push Hands–an ancient combat training deepened to a bodily meditation of giving and receiving–being active and being receptive....When we go back to our homes again our bodies will carry the lessons into our everyday activities..."

YOGA

IN THE WEST, THE WORD "YOGA" IS GENERALLY TAKEN TO MEAN the physical exercises of Hatha Yoga. Teachers of Hatha Yoga, however, generally recognize their skill to be one integral phase of the eight steps of yoga elaborated by Patanjali in his Yoga Sutras (see Raja Yoga, in The Way of Knowledge). Hatha Yoga teachers tend to focus on two of Patanjali's steps, the control of breath and posture, with the aim of awakening the subtle energy of the body, the life-force. In the yogic tradition this energy is known as kundalini and Kundalini Yoga—the discipline of awakening kundalini and channeling it through the body's vital centers in a controlled way—is the background to the practice of pranayama (breath control) and Hatha Yoga. There is in the yogic tradition an entire subtle physiology which provides the basis and the rationale for practice. The purpose of Kundalini Yoga is similar to the alchemical tradition of the West—the

Left & right: *The more subtle benefits of yoga will be experienced by all who practice it, whether their focus is on the spiritual or the purely physical.*

radical transformation of the physical body and the entire person through the unification of the male and female forces within the human force-field. This marriage is brought about by drawing the kundalini, which normally lies dormant at the base of the spine, up through subtle nerve channels and vital centers known as chakras to the crown of the head, where it awakens the dormant areas of the brain.

The chakras are vortices of psychic energy which lie at different points along the spinal column. Subtle channels (nadis) fan out from each chakra to different areas of the body, carrying prana–life force–backwards and forwards like a flow of alternating current in electric wires. The base chakra, in the pelvic floor, controls the survival and sexual instincts; the second chakra, at the tail of the spine, controls the unconscious; the third, at the solar plexus, is the primary seat of the ego and self-will; the fourth, in the chest, is the center of devotion and openness; the fifth, at the throat, controls speech and creativity; the sixth chakra is the "third eye," with its potential for intuitive knowledge. And the seventh chakra, at the crown of the head, is the seat of cosmic awareness.

The kundalini is raised through a central channel in the spine. As it passes through the chakras it awakens their potential and brings the two fundamental forces in the body–life force and consciousness–into union. Hinduism represents this mythologically in the marriage of Shiva and Shakti. Shakti, the female power, travels up the spine to become one with Shiva, who waits at the crown of the head.

The most common and direct method of awakening the kundalini is by the practice of pranayama, breath control. Through exercises of holding the breath, breathing forcefully, breathing in and out of different nostrils alternately, the practitioner not only increases the flow of prana through the body but creates a "fire" which heats the

kundalini and awakens it. Pranayama is practiced in conjunction with a variety of "asanas"–Hatha Yoga postures–to ensure that the prana is directed along the proper course.

The application of this psychospiritual background to yoga may or may not be put into practice by the individual. For every person who practices yoga as a serious spiritual path, there will be a hundred who use it as a means of toning up and relaxing. Either motive is perfectly valid. Yoga and pranayama have direct physical effects on health and well-being that can be of real benefit to people who have no interest in the farther reaches of yoga philosophy.

Because the physical body is not separate from the rest of our being, yoga will automatically act in ways that are not simply physical. The body is a flow of forces, not a piece of machinery. Breathing plays a central role in our every movement, thought, activity and feeling; when we are upset, depressed, angry or unusually happy, our breathing patterns change. Any alteration in breathing pattern in turn affects our state of mind; unacknowledged feelings may surface, or old memories and sensations. When the breathing rhythm is stabilized, our thoughts and feelings stabilize too.

Breathing control usually accompanies the asanas of Hatha Yoga because the quality of breathing affects every movement we make. The external movement is synchronized with inhaling or exhaling, depending on the activity. Forward bending and twisting movements occur most easily during exhalation, while backward bending is facilitated by inhalation. Attention to the breath in this way, in conjunction with a posture, will bring with it the quality of mindfulness that is cultivated in meditation. By focusing on physical sensation as we breathe and hold a yoga posture, we are able to develop a witness consciousness. We learn to tolerate the direct experience of life without having to escape it or change it in any way.

KRIPALU CENTER
FOR YOGA AND HEALTH

*You must approach your yoga practice with
reverence and gratitude and love. It's very much
like entering a temple.*

Amrit Desai

THE KRIPALU CENTER, NEAR LENOX, MASSACHUSETTS, IS A magical place with evergreen forests and walking trails on the edge of Lake Mahkeenac. It was founded by Yogi Amrit Desai in 1983 and named after his master, Swami Kripalvanandji, known and revered in India as one of the greatest masters of Kundalini Yoga. Amrit met his master when he was just sixteen and stayed with him until 1960 when, at the age of twenty eight, he moved to the USA to study at the Philadelphia College of Art.

Amrit quickly became an award-winning artist and textile designer; but even in the midst of his success, his real love–the practice of yoga–took more and more of his time and attention. After further study in India with his master, in 1966 he decided to devote all his

energies to yoga and founded the Yoga Society of Pennsylvania. In 1970, during his routine morning yoga practice, Amrit experienced a spiritual awakening that proved to be a landmark in his personal transformation. His master called him to India to give him the highest initiations and it was on his return that his students, aware of the profound shift in his energy, began to call him "Gurudev," meaning "beloved teacher."

Gurudev's awakening transformed both his life and his yoga. He developed a whole new approach to Hatha Yoga which he called Kripalu Yoga Meditation in Action. He likens yoga to a bird whose body is spirit and whose two wings are respectively will and surrender. The bird soars when the two wings are working together.

Left: *The Kripalu Center for Yoga and Health.*

Right: *Yogi Amrit Desai.*

The practice of will is the practice of purification. Kripalu yoga includes moral and ethical advice along the lines of Patanjali's sutras, attention to diet and the practice of Hatha Yoga and pranayama. The purpose is to develop a sense of ego that is not shaken by the world; good physical health, the capacity to express feelings clearly and a one-pointed mind that is not deterred from its balance by agitation. Gurudev's teacher called this "creating the fortress of the self."

Willful practice heightens our ability to "be with" sensations, thoughts, feelings, without having to do anything–without manipulating the external world to change the experience and without having to shut down or dissociate in order to avoid a painful state of mind or body. With time and experience, we begin to develop faith that as we remain aware and in balance, our energy or prana will move in just the way it needs to for deep healing to occur. This is the beginning of the path of surrender, when one senses that integration will take place on its own. There is nothing to do, nothing to achieve, nowhere to go; just the staying with bodily experience from moment to moment, without repressing or expressing anything. Kripalu calls this "riding the wave" and gives a sequence to follow: breathe, relax, feel (become aware of the feelings in the body), watch, allow. A particular style of asana is also used to encourage prana to move freely through the body. This surrender is known at Kripalu as "Meditation in Motion," or posture flow, and is primarily letting go of the self-concept.

Kripalu Center offers a wide range of retreat programs throughout the year, including a fourteen day Chakra Yoga Retreat, retreats and yoga for men and women, and meditation retreats. You can also create your own spiritual retreat, absorb the peace and beauty of the Center, or come simply for rest and reflection. If you choose to create your own program, you can include two yoga classes daily, meditation and pranayama. There is also a Kripalu Health program with various body therapies available. Three nights minimum stay is required for a personal retreat.

YASODHARA ASHRAM YOGA RETREAT AND STUDY CENTER

WHEN SHE WAS A YOUNG GIRL AT BOARDING SCHOOL, SWAMI Radha had a vision of a temple. This vision returned to her many times over the years in dreams, each time becoming clearer, revealing more detail. The setting was always the same, with the temple overlooking a lake at the end of a long road. In later dreams she entered the temple and found many people there of all races and religions gathered around a glorious light.

Swami Radha, German by birth, went on to become the first Western woman to be initiated as a renunciate by Swami Sivananda, the great Kundalini Yoga teacher from Rishikesh, India. After her initiation, Sivananda told her to return to the West to spread the teachings. He told her to go to Canada, give lectures, start an ashram and to take no money for her work. She was to live on faith alone. In 1956 she arrived in Montreal penniless and with hardly any English. She followed her guru's instructions to the letter, opening her first ashram in Burnaby, British Columbia, in 1957. In 1963 she and seven young men came to

Kootenay Bay, a long, narrow, deep glacier lake in south-eastern British Columbia. The hundred acres they purchased there became the Yasodhara Ashram of today. There is now a large guest lodge, classrooms and the Temple of Divine Light which she saw in her visions, dedicated to the light in all religions.

Swami Radha's approach to yoga is unique: she blends the traditional Hatha Yoga asanas and pranayama with the Western

Left: *The meditation hall at the Yashoda Ashram.*

Below: *Swami Sivananda Radha, founder of the Yashoda Ashram.*

existence. The asanas, they begin to realize, are all connected to deeper levels of meditative awareness and evoke those levels.

In her book *Hatha Yoga–The Hidden Language*, Swami Radha encourages practitioners to ask themselves what the different names of the asanas mean to them personally. The asanas are traditionally grouped under headings like Mountain, Birds, Fish and Reptiles, Animals. Students are guided to discover for themselves the deeper meanings hidden in the names and postures of the asanas. She adopts the same approach in her book, *Kundalini–Yoga for the West*, which leads practitioners to their own personal insights into the significance of the chakras and of kundalini yoga.

The resident staff at Yasodhara offer guided retreats which include hatha yoga, mantra and chanting sessions and kundalini yoga. Guests may also create their own retreat and make use of the ashram facilities. Yasodhara can let you know about other, smaller retreat centers in USA, called Radha Houses.

characteristic of inquiry. Many people come to yoga in order to relax or tone their bodies. Then, as they stay with the practice, they make certain discoveries. They realize that they feel better physically. They begin to breathe and move more freely. Their concentration may improve. Something else begins to emerge: the sense that, though what they already experience is desirable, there must be something more. They begin to have an intuition about the deeper levels of their

THE WALK OF LIFE:

RETREATS WITH SUPRAPTO IN JAVA

SUPRAPTO IS A UNIQUE TEACHER OF FREE-FORM MOVEMENT IN Java. His work has been discovered in the last few years by a small but growing number of Westerners. He runs month-long retreats in October each year, working around six hours a day. A few Westerners now teach his work in Europe, usually in periods of up to five days. Helen Poyner was one of the first Westerners to work with Suprapto and she gives the following account of her time with him.

"Solo, an old cultural city in Central Java. The moist, still air is bright with sunshine in a garden of brilliant tropical greens. Under the vaulted roof of a beautiful pendopo a circle of people are sitting or lying, relaxed and silent. Fifteen Westerners and a small Javanese man with long dark hair.

"Later, bodies moving through the shady spaces of this vast open-sided hall. Bare feet slapping on the tiled floor, long legs reaching in giant strides, people leaping and running, shouts of joy, a shriek of

rage, someone standing motionless, eyes open, relaxed, alert... periodically... a voice speaking in Javanese English: "Yes, like that... no, no, too much in front... relax your back, physique, physique [be more physical]..."

"Suprapto, known simply as Prapto, is a Javanese artist and teacher who has been involved in different types of movement since childhood, including the martial arts and traditional Javanese dance. His work is unique and defies categorization. He is a Buddhist and one of the most formative influences on his work were the many years he spent working with his meditation teacher who, although not a movement teacher, helped Prapto to develop and refine his use of movement using the same tools he used to guide and check his meditation. This was coupled with years spent practicing movement, mostly alone, in any condition—outside, on the earth, with the plants, in the rain, with the wind and the sun. It is only in recent years that

Prapto has begun to share his work with others, specifically with Westerners–first with one, then a group of four and subsequently through workshops in Europe which led to these intensive programs in Java.

"One night Prapto asks the question, "What is the source of this work? Art? Religion? The martial arts?" We discuss different theories and the answer is not clear to me: they are all aspects of Prapto's background and all areas in which the work can be applied. Prapto does not see the work as something he has created but rather that it exists in its own right and that he serves the evolution of it, learning together with the people who come to him... When someone thanked him after a particularly powerful piece of work he said, "Don't give thanks for me, give thanks for life."

"He works with people in many different ways; sometimes just watching and guiding, other times moving with them, encouraging them in a certain direction or reflecting their movement through exaggerated mimicry. Sometimes he prays and chants, using movement and touch. Often he appears transformed when working with others, his own movement taking on very different qualities, of a wild animal, a child, or a fighter. When asked how he works with people he merely replied that he works to see them more clearly and then does what comes. He is humble, offers suggestions as his opinion rather than as absolute truth and is open about his short-comings, not pretending to be more clear than he is. In this way he models the basic attitude that he asks of us in the work, to accept our own level–that is, to see ourselves as we are without blame or judgment, false humility or pride; to accept our limitations and also to be able to perceive others and our surroundings more clearly. It soon becomes clear that our attitude in movement is as important as the movement itself. But the focal point is always the body, even when practicing meditation.

"In movement terms, the work is delightfully simple. After over fifteen years as a movement student, artist and teacher, I was initially in danger of being very dismissive about some of the simple exercises we were given, such as moving through space down to the floor, on the floor and up again; or working in pairs, leading and following; or with an object. What was so special? I had done such exercises many times before. Yet even in the early stages... it was clear that these exercises worked on a deeper level than is usual, both in terms of the quality of movement released and in terms of the internal experience of the participants.

"Relaxation, even in activity, was the keynote of the work–not to be confused with "spacing out," or collapsing. Relaxation in the sense that a cat can be totally relaxed and yet physically available to any demand that may be made of it. At the same time the importance of accepting our level in relaxation was stressed, rather than imposing a false relaxation on top of a deeper layer of tension. It was a question of being relaxed in our attitude even when there was tension.

"The work has no form in the sense that Tai Chi, ballet, or highly stylized classical Javanese dance, has form. How you do something, the quality of your presence and authenticity in a movement, is more important than the form of the movement. In terms of movement language, almost anything is possible. There are, however, basic elements that are returned to whatever the level of work. Prapto would often take us through sequences of walking, stopping, crawling and lying, surprising us with the different order, rhythm and speed of the instructions, testing our ability to be relaxed in any position and to stay present in the movement, always following rather than breaking the flow. Again and again we were reminded of the three stages: staying, preparing and walking. Staying in the sense of being still, taking a rest; walking including many different ways of moving through the space; and preparing being the transition between these two states. There was an emphasis on our contact with the ground and with our surroundings. We worked with our eyes open, seeing what was in front of us; the floor, a flower, another person. The challenge was neither to get lost in our own inner world, nor to be pulled away from our contact with ourselves by what was around us. In other words, to be at home in our body but with the windows and doors open.

"From these basic elements each individual's movement developed very differently. Often we would be left very much to our own resources while practicing, with occasional guidance or reminders

from Prapto, particularly if we were moving without real contact to the body, spinning off instead into thoughts, emotions, or fantasies.

"The lack of form plus the simplicity of the work make it both powerful and revealing. It is a stripping away, a paring down to essentials both on a personal and on a movement level. Form in movement provides one with a certain sense of security from which one can build or express. Prapto sees working without form as a more difficult and lengthy task because one has to find this security in oneself. That means going back to basics, to a meeting with oneself without any disguises or props. The struggle was to move with integrity, not for aesthetic effect or as a result of will, not to do anything unnecessary or untruthful and yet at the same time not to get stuck in immobility, questioning the authenticity of every impulse. If I tried to solve or understand the problems posed by the work conceptually while working, I became completely stuck. That is where the practice of the "simple walk" is so important: it brings one back to the body and to a way of solving the problem on a physical level.

"After we had worked for some weeks in Solo, just as I was beginning to feel some security in the work... we were taken to three very different environments to continue our practice. We spent three days working in each location: on a hilltop where Prapto has a simple Buddhist shrine; in an historic Hindu fertility temple in the mountains and on the shoreline of the Indian Ocean. Beautiful and challenging places to work. How to remain centered even when the earth is literally sliding away beneath one's feet, as it was in the sand-dunes? How to respond physically rather than imaginatively or associatively to one's surroundings, or to move in relation to the wind without being taken over by it or attempting to become one with it? "Wind is wind," Prapto would say, "Prapto is Prapto."

"At the end of the workshop, I felt that I was just beginning to grasp the basis of the work. At the same time it felt appropriate to stop, to have time to digest and to experience the effects in my daily life and creative work. This article can only be a personal statement of my understanding and experience of the work. Hours of discussion in Java pinpointed the difficulty of articulating its nature. It works through the body in a subtle way that touches the depths of one's being. It essentially needs to be experienced and understood through the body rather than in words."

THE WAY
OF ART

WHEN A MAN CHOOSES TO JOIN THE MONASTIC LIFE ON Mount Athos, in Greece, three different life styles will be open to him. He may join the monastery community, become a hermit, or become an icon painter. If he takes the latter course, he will spend his life in one of the several "skitis" on the holy mountain, in the company of a dozen other artist-monks. A "skiti" is a building the size of a farmhouse, whose community uses art as their principal spiritual practice. Their days are spent in the silent painting of icons, with the interior practice of the Jesus Prayer.

Iconography used to be practiced throughout Christianity, though today it is rare to find it in its traditional form outside Mount Athos. The artist followed a predetermined design which has barely altered in centuries. Like most pre-Renaissance art, it was anonymous, embodying not so much the work of an individual as the mark of the tradition itself. To deviate from the tradition would constitute a gross challenge to ecclesiastical authority and would be considered tantamount to heresy. Strict formulae determining color, ratio and size, as well as subject matter, continue to be followed today in the remaining icon studios of the Orthodox and Coptic churches.

These studios and the skitis of Mount Athos are the last vestiges in the West of what was once a world-wide attitude to art that saw making things to be a natural expression and celebration of the sacred. There was no word in the Middle Ages for what we now understand as art; then, as in traditional societies throughout time, art was not conceived as an act of creativity distinct from anything else. Everyone who worked with their hands, including painters and sculptors, were simply

Below: Seven Generations—
a sculpture by Frederick Franck.

Previous pages:
Through art we can express our
innermost thoughts and feelings.

Right: *Religious practice*
celebrated through art: here, a
monk paints icons for his church.

workmen. The idea that there was an un-bridgeable gap between worker and artist only occurred in the Renaissance, with the struggles of individuals like Leonardo and Michelangelo to have painting and sculpture admitted to the so-called liberal arts.

The medieval absorption of art into everyday activities lingers on in present day Bali. The Balinese have no word for art. They say instead that "they do all things as well as possible." They are a culture of amateurs (amatore–lover) rather than professionals. Everyone dances, sings, makes music or paints as an expression of life's creativity. For the Balinese, as for the icon painter, self-expression has little or nothing to do with art; whatever is created always has a religious or social function, rather than a personal one.

In the far East many arts and crafts are undertaken as specific ways to the Buddhist ideal of no-mind, the condition of unity in which there is no separation between subject and object. Almost any activity can be practiced in a way which encourages this condition of being; Zen Buddhists in China and Japan have over centuries developed the martial arts, calligraphy, haiku and music specifically for this purpose. The form of the art was less important than the state of mind it could engender. The form, then, was dispensable; a painting or a haiku would often be thrown away as soon as it was completed. In the same way, Balinese

music is never written down, even today; once a composition has served its purpose it is invariably discarded.

How different from the view of art and the artist that has prevailed in the West from the Renaissance until now. The discovery of perspective gave pride of place to the individual observer, whose point of view set him apart from the rest of the world. His painting, from the Renaissance onwards, is framed, separating it from the world around it. It now becomes an art-object, transportable and therefore collectable, an object of private rather than civic possession; ultimately, an investment.

Some commentators feel that we are unlikely to see great artists in the old Renaissance mold again. More and more people are wanting to make art of their own, rather than just stare at someone else's. More artists today wish to serve a community rather than work in isolation. Some, like Andy Goldsworthy, making sculpture out of twigs and leaves, ice or sand, have rejected the gallery system; others, like Peter Brook, have returned theater to its religious roots. The real shift, John Lane suggests in his book, *Art and the Sacred*, is in the underlying concept we have of the arts themselves: "…If poetry and painting, music and theater, will have little more to give as "arts," perhaps they will have much to give as modes of self-discovery, awareness and

personal exploration; as aids to the rediscovery of being and existence. Expansion of awareness could become the final end of all creative work. As Kathleen Raine says,... what is to come may be a beginning of a new age in which people will, as in the monastic middle ages–only differently–work on themselves; it is, after all, the only final usefulness of "works of art" to enable us to do so."

The purpose of most art retreats available today is to provide a context and an art form through which the individual may know and celebrate the deeper levels of life that exist in himself and in all things. This, not the creation of an individual work of art that can be admired by others, is the point of taking such a retreat. People can wake up in any number of ways and the art retreat is one such way, suitable perhaps for those who are more at ease with a pencil or brush in hand than with sitting on a meditation cushion. In an art retreat, the art is the meditation, in the same way that pouring tea or firing the arrow is the meditation practice of those who follow those ways. The contemporary art retreat is an echo of those pre-Renaissance times when art was a celebration of the unity of life itself; when the "artist" was a vehicle for a creative wellspring which he would never think to attribute to himself. This is the attitude Frederick Franck is referring to when he says of his retreats: "Instead of the pleasures of so-called self-expression, you will discover a greater one: the joy of letting a leaf, a branch, express itself, its being, through you. In order to reach that point you'll have to allow yourself to see that which you are drawing, whether leaf, plant, or weed, as the most important thing on earth, worthy of your fullest, deepest attention."

THE AWAKENED EYE

AN ART RETREAT WITH FREDERICK FRANCK

All that is, is worthy of being
drawn and what I have not drawn
I have never really seen.

Frederick Franck

FREDERICK FRANCK IS AN EXTRAORDINARY MAN. HE HOLDS degrees in dentistry, medicine and fine arts. He served for three years with Doctor Albert Schweitzer at Lambarene; he was the only artist to record all four sessions of the Second Vatican Council; he has written books on Africa and his years with Schweitzer, on Eastern and Western spiritual experience, on the mystic Angelus Silesius and several on seeing/drawing as meditation, including *The Zen of Seeing*. His drawings and paintings are part of many museum collections, including The Museum of Modern Art, The Whitney Museum and the Tokyo National Museum.

He gave his first "Zen of Seeing" retreat in the nineteen-seventies at Pacem in Terris, "the transreligious oasis of inwardness" that he built almost single-handedly on the remains of an eighteenth century water mill near where he lives with his wife, Claske, in Warwick, New York. He was 85 in 1994 and as active as ever. One of his sculptures, *The Unkillable Human*, was carried into Sarajevo in 1994 by an international group of women who risked their lives to reach the town for a peace conference organized with the women of Sarajevo. For Frederick Franck, "there is no other valid reason for drawing than the awareness of the eye awakening from its half-sleep. There is–I am

convinced—no other good reason for art, all the art-popes and theories notwithstanding..."

The two main elements of the retreat are seeing and silence. Participants are silent from beginning to end; even personal introductions are dispensed with. The point of the silence is to facilitate seeing and to allow the judging mind to come to rest. As preconceptions and judgments fall away, it becomes possible to see a clump of grass, a flower, a piece of wood, for what it is. Instead of trying to "be creative," to be original, or to make art objects, the aim is to arrive at a condition of trust in what the eyes see and to give one's full attention to the object to be drawn. One may draw the same piece of wood all day, so as to see the progression in the deepening act of seeing.

Franck offers no technique and does not assume the role of drawing teacher. Any word he may offer will be to indicate some weakness in the act of seeing. The retreat is a process not of learning so much as unlearning, of taking the scales of habit from one's eyes. Participants come to see that things exist only in their particulars, never in their generalities; that only this particular man or woman, this blade of grass, is real. In his retreat, the seeing is the meditation. Franck describes the first moments of his retreat thus.

Left:
Hiroshima: the Unkillable
Human —*a sculpture by
Frederick Franck.*

Opposite:
Risen Christ —*a sculpture by
Caroline Mackenzie.*

Previous pages:
142. Frederick Franck at work.

*143. In order to paint a leaf, it
is first necessary to truly see it.*

"Begin with something "simple," a leaf for instance. Take it in your hand and observe it closely for a few minutes. Then put it in a corner of your drawing paper, close your eyes... try to visualize it. Hold your pencil loosely and let it rest on the paper. After a few minutes of trying to visualize the leaf, open your eyes. You may now begin to see the leaf and while keeping fully concentrated on it, let your pencil start to move. As it moves, have the feeling that the pencil point is gently caressing the contours of the leaf: the outline that goes around it, as well as the cross-contours that go across it." A little later, he warns us that "there will be moments during the day when you will feel desperate to the point of wanting to quit. You may even tell yourself that you are bored. I have found out that these moments of despair often come when at last the ego gives up trying. It is the point where real seeing, where 'meditation' can start."

The day proceeds in this way, with Franck giving advice to everyone in turn without expecting an answer. The drawings are numbered in sequence, not signed and are displayed all together at the end of the day. When, at the end, someone exclaims that they cannot believe they drew what they did–that they always thought they couldn't draw–and where should they go from here, Franck gives the reply: "Just go on as you did today for fifteen years or so... Each deepened awareness leads to the next level of awareness. Instead of becoming blunted and cynical by existence, your sensitivity will become ever keener."

EXPLORING COSMIC IMAGES:
A RETREAT WITH CAROLINE MACKENZIE

IN 1974, AFTER COMPLETING A FINE ARTS DEGREE IN LONDON, Caroline Mackenzie went to India to study the symbolism of Hindu temples. Her own work in London had consisted of intensely personal water-color paintings, full of symbols that she herself could not understand, too interior to show her tutors. The prevailing college ethos had little time for interiority: it considered visionary artists such as William Blake technically incompetent and so hardly worth studying. Caroline changed to sculpture and found resonances with her own inner life in the sensuous and subtle world of Hindu symbols, which she discovered through the Indian sculpture in the British Museum.

She spent three months touring the Indian temple towns and during this time stayed briefly with an Indian Christian artist, Jyoti, and his wife. In contrast to the fiercely individualistic art world of her college, Jyoti worked in relationship to the community of the Indian church and the key to his creativity seemed to lie in its relatedness to society, to nature, to his own inner search and to God. Her visit to the village of this artist's family was to expand into six years. During this time she learned less about technique than the meaning and purpose inherent in the technique and applied what she learned to a series of carvings of traditional Hindu images. Her understanding of symbolism, psychology and religion underwent a profound change and she realized that she was acquiring a language through which to articulate her own inner experiences. The Nandi bull image, for example, which is found facing the holy of holies in a Shiva temple, is a symbol for our animal nature, which can be transformed through devotion to the

Lord; this image awakened in her a sense of the sacredness of the human body, with all its ambiguities and passions.

After six years in this Christian village, Caroline decided to enter the Hindu world more deeply and moved to Melkote, an ancient Sri Vaishnava pilgrimage center near Mysore. She studied Sanskrit and stayed another six years in this traditional Brahmin setting, becoming painfully aware of the injustices of the caste system and how difficult it would be for any Westerner to fully enter into the Hindu faith and culture. It was in Melkote that she began to see Christian imagery everywhere within the Hindu setting. She began to overcome her lifelong resistance to Christian symbols and to see her familiar cultural framework in a more universal perspective. While she was living in Melkote, a Christian ashram near Mysore asked her to make a set of Stations of the Cross to hang on coconut trees. She based each design on symbolism derived from the coconut tree blended with various motifs from her earlier work with Indian symbols. Then she was asked

to collaborate with Jyoti on the design for a church/temple for another Christian ashram. After fourteen years in India, Caroline returned to the West as a member of the Indian church. For her, Indian Christianity is a cross-cultural liberation: it places the Judaic prophetic tradition, in which God may intervene on behalf of the oppressed, in the context of a broader, cosmic awareness that celebrates the sacredness of all living things. It also gives her a way of understanding herself as a woman within a religious symbol system and of finding a proper relationship between art, society and Self. Since her return, she has been sharing her own cross-cultural exploration through art retreats whose theme is the cosmic dimension of symbols. The following is her account of the retreats she holds: Exploring Cosmic Images.

"While it is possible to describe symbols, their transformative power happens at an intuitive level. In an art retreat of this kind, the intention is to find a way into an experience of incarnation through art work, liturgy/ritual and meditation. By restricting the scope to three

Right & far right: *Work flowing from its environment: carvings by Caroline Mackenzie.*

Previous pages:
Baptism: Cosmic Christ—*a stained glass window designed by Caroline Mackenzie.*

particular symbols–the Tree of Life, the Indian Temple and the human body–we can approach our themes from different angles in a multi-layered way. Our overall purpose is to foster the process of personal integration within the context of a religious journey, using the symbols as our raw material.

"Participants range from those who consider themselves "post-Church" although still Christian, Buddhist and New Age seekers, as well as Christians of various denominations. The range of artistic ability stretches from those who can "hardly draw a straight line" to professional artists. I shall describe a particular retreat that I held at The Rowan Tree Center, in the valley of the river Wye, in Wales.

"On the Friday evening, I introduced the whole process of symbol making. We considered how the cave and the mountain form the basis for the Hindu temple and looked at the same type of movement, inwards and upwards, in the image of Jonah in the whale and Moses on the mountain. The whale is a cave, womb, or tomb and the mountain is like the tower of the temple. The image of the tree serves as a link between the dark earth and the bright sky. I ended the evening with some slides of a concrete example of symbols at work in the Inter-Faith meditation hall at Sameeksha, a center for Indian spirituality in South India.

"Saturday morning began with a half-hour meditation and at 8.00AM participants were invited to assemble on the lawn where a double-entranced labyrinth had been marked out with stones. At the center was an Indian oil-lamp in the form of a stylized tree. Then there was a liturgy involving a meditative procession into and out of the labyrinth reciting a litany in which the Creator was named as feminine.

"After breakfast, we examined the Tree of Life through a joint painting exercise and I gave a short explanation of the tree symbol in various traditions. Large sheets of newsprint were then stuck onto the wall and I divided the space horizontally into three equal parts. We then painted a large tree, with the roots in the lowest third, the trunk in the middle and the branches in the top. Later, we met under an old sycamore tree and I asked each person to find a tree with which s/he felt some empathy. After ten minutes they came together again and I gave a guided meditation in which participants closed their eyes,

planted their feet firmly on the ground and enacted the passage of his or her tree through the seasons. Then everyone did a painting of their particular tree. Later in the afternoon, I gave a slide presentation on the Hindu temple and at 6.30PM we met under the sycamore tree for evening liturgy. This particular retreat happened over Midsummer's Eve and we incorporated this into the symbolism. We processed in silence up the nearby hill and made a small fire there. There were readings from the Vedas, Celtic sources and a litany for Saint John the Baptist, whose feast is celebrated near midsummer, after which the sun will decrease. John, too, said he must decrease in order that Christ would increase. For that whole liturgy we consciously used masculine language and symbols, as in the morning the symbols and the language had been feminine.

"Sunday morning began in the chapel with meditation and after breakfast I gave a slide show and talk on "The Body Divine." I discussed how in Indian culture all bodies, male as well as female, are seen as appropriate to represent nature, while in the West a division is often made between woman as nature and man as culture. I showed pictures of *The Feminine Face of God*, by the Indian Christian artist Lucy D'Souza. I showed my own carvings of the Stations of the Cross, which show the journey of Christ to Calvary in terms of the suffering of the whole creation.

"The retreat closed with all of us building a sacred space on the lawn. It was based on the Inter-Faith meditation hall which I had described on the first night. Each person built one part and the whole process was completed in silence. When it was complete, we came together round it and the lamp at the center was lit. We processed "inside" the space and each person sat or squatted facing the lamp at the center. Our final meditation started with three chimes on the cymbals and ended with chanting "Om" three times."

THE WAY
OF SOUND

*God respects me when I work
but loves me when I sing.*

Rabindranath Tagore

THE EARS ARE THE FIRST SENSE ORGAN TO AWAKEN, FOR THE fetus can hear in the dark of the womb; and hearing is the last sense to fade away at death. Human beings were made to be vocal and listening creatures. Sound, especially that of the human voice, has power. It is no primitive whim that makes the men of the Dogon tribe in Mali whisper in the ear of their women before lying with them to conceive a child. Nor is it mere medieval fantasy that depicts the Annunciation as a stream of golden light pouring from the Angel Gabriel into the ear of the Virgin Mary. It was with wise words, too, that the serpent awoke the soul of Eve in the Garden.

The Word brings forth life, creativity, our deepest longings and desires. Sound has been used in every religious tradition since time immemorial. From the individual incantations of the tribal shaman, through the chants and mantras of Hinduism and Buddhism, the early

Opposite: *As people chant together, their heart beats fall into synchronization: trance states may result.*

Previous pages:
150. Stringed instruments can create intensely sweet resonances and harmonics, opening the space for internal reflection.

151. Rabindranath Tagore, who won the Nobel Prize for literature in 1913.

Christian plain song and Gregorian chant, the human family has developed a sophisticated awareness of sound which is being rediscovered and applied in new ways today. The Hindu yogi knows which "seed sound" to intone in order to awaken the power of any particular chakra and how to create different mental states and psychophysical energies by using the appropriate mantra. A Native American shaman knows which sounds to make for healing, while the low chanting of Japanese or Tibetan Buddhist monks generates primordial stillness in both practitioner and listener. The long-held belief that the human voice is the most powerful of all instruments is borne out in recent research at the University of Paris on the effect of sound on premature babies. The criterion was how far each selection of music could calm the disturbed rhythm typical of a premature infant and bring its heartbeat back to a firm, regular and slow rhythm.

Of all the types of music investigated, the most effective was the mother's own voice singing to her baby; the second was traditional women's singing from the Hebrides; the third was a male voice in the Abbey of Le Thoronet, in Provence. The sound of the ocean also slowed the heartbeat but as soon as this sound stopped the heartbeat returned to its chaotic state; with the three types of human singing, the effect continued after the music had stopped. Iegor Reznikoff, Professor of Art and Music of Antiquity at the University of Paris, suggests that this is because human consciousness is structured by the human voice, even before birth; the voice penetrates deeply into the layers of human consciousness itself (see *Caduceus Magazine*). Music with very steady, strong pulsation and repetitive rhythms can alter the rhythms of our heartbeat, respiration and brainwaves through a process known as "entrainment," bringing them into synchronization with that pulsation. A group of singers who are "in tune" will be found to have the same pulse rate; in the same way, Tibetan Buddhist chanting will bring the community of monks to a state of "one mind and body." As well as having beneficial effects on the individual, "sounding" in this way brings a deeply-felt sense of community. It is no accident, then, that song has always played a major part in traditional community life everywhere in the world.

The last ten years has seen a renaissance of interest and research into the effects of sound: its power to heal, to energize, and to be a path to spiritual wholeness. Traditionally, the use of the singing voice to generate spiritual insight and devotion was practiced within a specific religious context: only a monk, for example, would be trained in the Tibetan chanting practices, which are part of a much wider body of esoteric knowledge. Today, singing and chanting practices that were once secret are now being taught in a variety of non-religious contexts. Often, leaders of voice workshops and retreats (including the two whose work is discussed below) have been trained in a particular form of spiritual practice which includes voice training.

Their work is subsequently based on a personal experience of a body of spiritual knowledge. There is now a wide range of retreats to cater for the growing interest in sound and voice, and many of these are inspired by one or other spiritual tradition. They include chanting retreats, free-form voice retreats, creative voice and singing retreats, and healing sound retreats.

Chanting is usually the repetition of short phrases of tones and the most common forms known today derive from the Hindu and Buddhist traditions. Our verb to "enchant" reminds us of the essential purpose of this kind of singing–it is intended to take the practitioner into a magical or mystical state of mind. Chanting is used to enter the various degrees of trance state, or absorption, in which one loses ordinary consciousness. It is also used to induce a condition of enhanced clarity and energy, so that the individual feels more real and alive than he was before; and it is used to open the heart, to allow the feeling life to flow.

In India, different mantras are used for evoking various feeling states. Lama Govinda speaks of the mantra as being a pre-linguistic, primordial sound which expresses feeling but not concept. The most powerful of all mantras is the sound "Om." "Whoever speaks this mantra thirty five million times," it says in the Upanishads, "the mantra of the sacred word... shall be freed of all his bonds and shall reach

Left: *Retreatants at the Kagyu Center, France, participate in a chanting ceremony.*

The Tibetans chant this mantra harmonically, producing entire chords with a single human voice. This is known in the West as "overtoning" and several Western teachers who have mastered this art now teach it in their voice retreats. Joachim Ernst Berendt explains the overtone effect in his book, *Nada Brahma*.

"When a string is set vibrating (which is the archetype of all sound production), what vibrates is not only the entire string but also inevitably half of the string (the next higher octave, that is); as well as two-thirds of the string (the fifth), three quarters (the fourth), three fifths (the major sixth), four fifths (the major third), five sixths (the minor third) and so on. In other words, the entire scale is sounded but as an overtone scale... Each note contains all the others..." By cultivating all the overtones of a sound, the Tibetan monks constantly underline the context of every tone with the totality, "the cosmos of all tones." In this way they produce the impression of many-voiced

absolute liberty." For the sages of India and Tibet, the world is sound and the audible sound that comes closest to the primal sound of the world is "Om." Sounding and meditating on Om correctly is dependent on the proper method of breathing. Om "happens" while exhaling and signifies that point where breath becomes word and word becomes breath.

chords. To do this, all the parts of the body involved in creating the sound must be totally relaxed. Overtone singing is also practiced by the shamans of the Mongolian Tuvan in Siberia.

Early Christian and Gregorian chant is used in some contemporary retreats because the richness of the Latin vowel sounds, which are often stretched over many tones, create a highly purifying and energizing sound "medicine." This was made clear by an event reported by James D'Angelo in *Caduceus Magazine*. Dr. Tomatis, founder of The Tomatis Clinic in Paris, which uses sound for healing purposes, was called to a monastery by the abbot to diagnose the cause of the tiredness and lethargy of his monks. He discovered that the abbot had done away with the traditional daily schedule of chanting in order to gain time for other things. Tomatis recommended that the chanting be reinstated and within a few months the monks regained their full energy with their usual minimum of sleep. For the Pythagoreans, it was signified by the word, "harmonia." On one of the columns of the tenth century abbey church of Cluny, in France, is written the motto: "The Octave teaches all Saints to be Blessed." The knowledge of the Cluny monks was used in their infirmary; there are detailed accounts of the musical ways in which the dying were tended. Music was used to transform the pain which might prevent anyone from a blessed death—an ancient tradition known earlier to Gregory the Great who, in 604CE, wrote that "singing helps the soul to part well from the body." Similar work is being carried out today at the Saint Patrick Hospital in Missoula, Montana, where Therese Schroeder-Sheker runs a department of Music Thanatology with twenty-seven harps and resident singing harpists.

Iegor Reznikoff has developed a practice of sound healing which has developed out of his work with early Christian chant at the University of Paris. He has worked with mentally disabled people, with those in a comatose state (some of who have been brought to consciousness by someone singing by them) and with mothers giving birth. With people in a normal physiological condition, his aim is to bring harmony between consciousness and specific parts of the body through sound. Certain sounds relate directly to particular parts of the body; if you put your hand on your chest and chant "aa," for example, you feel the vibration there; "oo" resonates in the throat, mouth and lower part of the face and "mm" on the top of your head. Generally, when a person has a poor consciousness of a particular part of their body, they will also have a weak sound perception of these parts. Chanting the appropriate sound becomes the best way to recover consciousness of that part of the body.

Of all practices, the use of the singing/chanting voice most directly serves as a bridge between the physical and spiritual domains. Whether a voice retreat teaches you a particular skill like overtoning, or the release of creativity through spontaneous singing and sounding, the result will always include a tangible sense of "harmonia," of enhanced aliveness and connectedness with oneself.

THE HEALING VOICE:

A RETREAT WITH JILL PURCE

JILL PURCE PIONEERED THE REDISCOVERY OF ANCIENT VOCAL techniques, the power of group chant and the potential of the voice as a magical instrument for healing and meditation. She has taught in America and Europe for twenty years, teaching diverse forms of sacred chant, especially the Mongolian overtone chanting. She is the author of *The Mystic Spiral: Journey of the Soul*. She is married to the biologist, Rupert Sheldrake. Here, she describes her retreat in her own words.

"My aim is not modest. I am trying to re-enchant the world, which means to make it magical through chanting. My retreat-style residential workshops have this as their aim. I am trying to reintroduce into our daily lives ways of experiencing the extraordinary and ancient power of group chant. My aim is to help people rediscover their own voices as tools for deep meditation and personal transformation.

"There is a profound sense of disenchantment in Western society. I think people feel like this because quite literally there is no chant in

their lives. All the situations in which people came together in traditional cultures to chant have gradually eroded away, so people feel disempowered and helpless in a desacralized world. My aim is to re-enchant the world, to make it more magical through people chanting together again. The retreat gives us a real sense of what a literally enchanted community could be like.

"My own first transmission of the power of the voice came in early childhood in Ireland. We were visiting a remote island off the West coast. The only other people in the small boat were the old women of the island returning home. A violent storm blew up and it seemed obvious to all of us that we were going to drown. Suddenly the women began to sing with an ancient power and deep passion. Almost at once our fear was transformed into strength and a sense of control, until we were overcome with feelings of bliss and enchantment.

"During the retreat week we work with increasing intensity and at deeper and deeper levels, touching quite often on areas of the psyche

long buried. Through the therapeutic use of the voice we are able to bring these areas of hurt and pain safely up to the surface into the light of clarity and illumination, often ridding ourselves of traumas which have beset us since early childhood.

"One of the effects of chanting is the dissolution of boundaries and when this happens something new can take place in the psyche and body of a person. Chanting seems to directly stimulate the emission of certain chemicals in the brain, such as endorphins, which give rise to enhanced awareness, blissful calm and other deep meditative states.

"People of all ages and backgrounds come together for these retreats. I have people from eleven to ninety, from professional musicians, singers and therapists who want to extend their work, to those who were told at school they could not sing in tune. The retreats also attract people who want to work on emotional or physical blocks, as well as professional educators, actors and healers. People often report miraculous healing experiences: headaches and backache may suddenly vanish, or emotional burdens quickly lift. Others report feeling more confident and powerful. Overtone chanting, in particular, can facilitate visionary experiences.

"My teaching begins with instruction in a specific form of breathing. This is the basis of all the other work. We then begin to tune our voices together and discover the effect of the voice on the body, mind and spirit. We learn exactly what the voice does and its power to heal.

"A specific skill I teach is Mongolian overtone chanting. This involves a single note only but by modulating all the resonant cavities, including the shape of the mouth, you make audible, high, bell-like sounds which float above the continuous bass note in a way which makes people think of the music of the spheres. The overtones are the component parts of the fundamental note being chanted and are normally too quiet to be audible. Here they are filtered in such a way that they can be heard louder than the note itself. It is a powerful experience even to listen to it, producing a state of extreme calm and clarity.

"One of the practices I have been exploring most intensely during the retreat week is the healing of the ancestral lines. We go back through our families and by means of the voice we exorcise family curses, unacknowledged deaths, redundant themes and patterns, other ancient hurts. At the same time, we uncover the particular blessings, the gifts which we receive from our ancestors. Often, we

find what the Native Americans call "our medicine," the gift which we are to the world and how this relates to the essence of our family patterns. One person who did this work said that they had managed to release and heal their relationship with their mother, which had been untouched by years of therapy.

"Depending on the time of year, we do ceremonies which mark the passing seasons and reflect and interact with the quality of time, making accessible the spirits of the moment, so that we can remain in harmony with it. In a similar way we work with the spirits of the place, learning to interact with the forces and spirits of nature and understand how they interface with our lives and how they can have a benign influence on us. We discover how these forces affect our place of birth, our childhood and the health of our family lines; and what we can do

to balance these forces of nature and bring our lives into harmony with them. In addition to these, we do different purification practices and work with the elements to purify past and future karma and balance the energies in our bodies. I also work with dreams through sound and mantra. I use chant combined with ceremonial dance to connect with one of the most ancient forms of healing, the power of vocally induced trance. We do many ancient forms of sacred chant.

"Underlying all my work is the premise that the voice is a key to spiritual transformation. Because the sound of the voice is directly linked through the breath to the activities of the mind, through working with the voice we can learn to enter the state the Tibetans know as "rigpa," the awareness which combines emptiness with clarity. This leads ultimately to illumination."

THE NAKED VOICE:

RETREATS WITH CHLOË GOODCHILD

Listen to the voice inside you
She is waiting to be found
Once you've heard that sound inside you,
You will always stand your ground.

Chloë Goodchild, The Naked Voice

CHLOË GOODCHILD'S WORK WITH THE VOICE ARISES FROM the alchemy of her own life: from a fusion of her training in voice and music with her personal spiritual journey. She studied Music and Drama at Cambridge, discovered the primal sounds of Africa during a year in Kenya and studied Indian vocal practices with Gilles Petit, a French musician whose work bridges Eastern and Western styles. Brought up in the family of an Anglican bishop, she discovered her own spiritual home in India, especially in the person of the woman saint, Ananda Mayi Ma and the sage of Arunachala, Ramana Maharshi.

The voice has become for her a metaphor for the expression of spiritual values in everyday life. She says that "the voice inside each of us is the voice that speaks and sings our truth. By learning to listen to our voice, by learning to honor, accept and express its message, we begin to discover our inner freedom and to carry it into the world." What she helps people to access in her retreats is the "inner call" that

exists behind the layers of the personality or conditioned self and also behind any of the vocal styles a person may have learned. This "secret sound" is the voice of one's own authenticity, from which true power, authority and love all stem. The singing voice is a vehicle for that authenticity to express itself. Goodchild calls herself a "creative practitioner" rather than an artist, in order to extend the whole concept of artistic practice out from the work of the professional specialist to include those people who want to commit themselves to the art of living itself, moment by moment. Her retreats serve as a context for developing that commitment and for expressing it through one's own unique voice—which for Goodchild herself, as well as for some of her students, means public performances of improvised sound and song.

The influence of the mystical Christian, Hindu and Buddhist traditions is evident in Goodchild's music. The chanting of mantram, Indian sacred hymns and early Christian modes, are the foundation of

her singing practice. Out of the group chanting arise the devotional songs of the heart. These in turn provide material for the improvised singing which follows. She sees simple improvisation as a first step away from the familiar structures of bar-lines and well-known tunes with clear-cut beginnings and endings, into the potential chaos and uncharted regions of the "heart sound." After singing free-form for a while, the singer often experiences an uprush of strong emotions, which lead to a realm of deeper feeling. At that moment, Goodchild encourages the practitioner to keep singing through the emotion,

until they reach a level of silence out of which they can continue singing. Slowly, the voice of the soul begins to reveal itself.

For her, the process of singing is meditative and passionate. Whatever the song or the sound, the aim is to allow it to arise from a deeper level of interior stillness. All kinds of people come to her retreats. Many are aspiring professional singers who want to have a broader spiritual context for their work and who want to develop the spontaneity and joy that are typical of Goodchild's own public performances. Others have always been afraid to sing, or feel they cannot sing in tune and want to

Left: *Chloë Goodchild in the desert: exploring silence through sound.*

Previous pages:
162. Chloë Goodchild, singing from her heart.

163. Chanting after meditation: the voice unites spirit with surroundings.

develop confidence in their own voice. People also come for the sense of spiritual community that a retreat engenders and the inspiration and energy that singing gives. While the work is oriented towards the individual, each singer is supported by the group's attention, which is developed as an integral part of the retreat.

"My retreats aim to give expression to a person's authentic voice," says Goodchild. "You can recognize the sound of that voice because it has a ring to it in which the whole body is resonating. It joins the higher and the lower; it brings a person into the singing heart. First we have to create the context in which this can happen and that context is awareness, a quality of attention in which people are 'present'. So I always begin the retreat with a period of silence, followed by the recitation of sacred chants, which establish an atmosphere of being. Within this atmosphere, true listening becomes possible. People go into pairs and practice listening both to the sound of their own speaking voice and to the other. While they are speaking, I ask them to hold the silent question, 'Who is speaking?' Later on in the retreat, the question becomes, 'Who is singing?'

"The initial exercises are all based on listening and self-inquiry. In the pairs exercise they share their 'vocal history', which I ask them to prepare before the retreat. This is an account of the memories they have of sound in their lives, including responses to and feelings about their own voice. Often, people feel during this exercise that they have been 'heard' for the first time in their lives.

"After various exercises of this kind, we dance and move and practice relaxation and breathing exercises, so that they can sing with the whole body, in a full-blooded way, from the belly right up to the heart. Then I sing to the group, in a way that is spontaneous and from the heart, without thought. This gives the group a deeper feeling for a way of sounding which arises out of a state of gratitude and self-acceptance. Later, I ask them to go alone into the outside environment (I always ensure the retreat is in quiet and beautiful natural surroundings) in order to listen to nature–to the wind, the rain, the leaves, the birds. Throughout, there are regular meditation sessions and times for silent reflection.

"By the second day, each person will have a song prepared that they will proceed to sing in various settings during the rest of the retreat–in couples, in small groups and eventually, alone in front of the whole group. They will be 'heard' throughout in a highly attentive atmosphere which is as important as the singing itself. The practice is to develop a listening faculty which is free of the ordinary judging mind. I encourage this listening with two fundamental principles which people learn to apply: acceptance of what is and gratitude for what is. When a person is listened to in this way, they are freed to sing and 'be' in a surrendered, open way which they may never have experienced before. Ultimately, the singer and the audience become one and the same. The audience is listening with the attitude that they are the singer and her voice and the singer is singing to an extension of herself. There becomes only one voice and one body. This is sacred performance and is the culmination of the retreat. What emerges from this is the experience of being real and its consequence of joy."

Chloë Goodchild's retreat schedule, along with her book and audio-cassette–both with the title of *The Naked Voice*–can be obtained from The Naked Voice Retreats.

THE WAY OF THE WILDERNESS

> *In wildness is the*
> *preservation of the world.*
>
> · Henry David Thoreau

W<small>E HAVE TAMED THE WILDNESS IN OUR CULTURE ALMOST TO</small> the point of extinction. More often than not, we speak of nature as if it were the exclusive preserve of either the conservationist or the romantic. We refer to the "ecosystem" as if nature were an extension of our living room, to be regulated, monitored and serviced at regular intervals, much like a central heating system.

Either that, or nature is mentioned in soft tones verging on the sentimental; she is our Mother from whom we have turned away and whom we need to learn to love again. These perspectives are not untrue but their overstatement runs the risk of depriving the natural world of its own power and vigor by reducing it to purely human terms.

Despite our worries and projections, Nature remains terrible and mighty, with impetuous and unpredictable moods that can strike fear into the heart of whole populations. Awe and dread (in the sense of holy fear) are natural responses to the wildness of Nature. When we lose touch with these primordial feelings, we lose touch with a sense of proportion about our place in the cosmos and when that happens, we lose touch with our souls.

A wilderness retreat returns us to our natural place. To walk in the wild with others for a period of time is to touch base with original human companionship, to feel the raw immensity of the planet we live on and to begin to know our own wildness that has lived in us all

along. We are dependent on reflexes, instincts and appetites that we are hardly aware of and that we cannot, or had better not, stop. Under the daily chatter of the psyche, we might hear in some unsuspecting moment the distant groan of a wild man or woman deep down inside us. As it becomes more difficult to find an acceptable place for this voice in our civilized life, it manifests as a brute which erupts blindly in meaningless violence and destruction.

Our wild selves are squeezed behind walls and fences into ever diminishing spaces. Yet we know that our needs depend on a balanced cooperation between the domestic and wilderness. Wendell Berry tells us "a forest or a crop, no matter how intentionally husbanded by human foresters or farmers, will be found to be healthy precisely to the extent that it is wild–able to collaborate with earth, air, light and water in the way common to plants before humans walked on the earth. We know from experience that we can increase our domestic demands upon plants so far that we force them into kinds of failure that wild plants do not experience. Breeders of domestic animals, likewise, know that when a breeding program is too much governed

by human intention... uselessness is the result. Size or productivity, for instance, will be gained at the cost of health, vigor, or reproductive ability. In other words, so-called domestic animals must remain half wild, or more than half, because they are creatures of nature." (Wendell Berry, *The Landscape of Harmony*.)

We humans are creatures of nature too. We forego our wildness at our peril. I suspect that the more we domesticate our more primal nature, the more we cut ourselves off from the bare truths of our soul and spirit. To go on a wilderness retreat is to return to our instincts and begin to open the sluice-gates through which the authentic feelings for life–awe, dread, wonder, marvel, joy–can pour.

We usually do not even hear the conversation between the instinctual side of our nature and Nature itself; yet it is a constant dialogue. Our hearts are always leaping out to the hills and the woodlands we pass through. This was so obvious in earlier times that people personified this exchange of energy and heard the trees speaking and the wind crying. In the Aeneid, Virgil breaks off a branch, blood comes out and the branch speaks.

Right & left: *The reflexes and instincts of wild animals must not be completely lost to our wild selves. We must re-learn lost habits, lost knowledges to re-integrate with the wildernesses within.*

Previous pages: *Vast expanses of wilderness offer immense opportunities to explore true solitude.*

This primal connection between humanity and nature starts to emerge within a few days of being out in the desert, on the mountain or the river; especially when the group is traveling in silence. A wilderness retreat differs from a trekking or adventure holiday not so much in its content (though often the content will be completely different) but in its context. The purpose of a trekking holiday might be to climb as many peaks as one can, or to get as many hours of walking as possible into the day. A wilderness retreat is not concerned with physical achievement but with mindful association with oneself, with others and with nature. Often a group will stroll, rather than walk intently, through the wildness surrounding it. The body and mind settles into a slower, more regular rhythm than city life allows; they become more open to the elemental forces around them and to the deeper callings within. People worry that they need to be fit to take a wilderness retreat but in practice they just need to be able to walk for a few hours each day and if they weren't fit to begin with, they will probably be so at the end–less because of the demanding schedule than because of the deeper nourishment their being has received.

JOURNEY INTO EMPTINESS:
THE SAHARA WALK

I RUN OCCASIONAL WALKING JOURNEYS IN THE SAHARA FOR THE Open Gate. This is an account of one that took place in southern Algeria in 1990. I am there to provide the context–morning meditation, evening sharing circles and the walking itself. The speaking, I leave to the wilderness. At the end of that November, we were in a plane circling over the region north of Niger, near the border with Libya. Our base was to be Djanet, a speck of a place far from anywhere. It is the same distance from London to Algiers as it is from Algiers to Djanet. The difference is that the second journey is all across desert.

It looked as if we were going to land in a sand dune. There was nothing else down there; no sign of habitation to be seen. Then, on our right, a huge mountain plateau rolled into view and at one stroke I could see across thousands of years. I could see deep ravines and gorges that great rivers and mountain streams had once cut into this massive table of rock and the skeletal remains of vegetation, trees and shrubs, victims of the recent drought and the tightening grip of the desert. As the plane leveled for landing, there was nothing to be seen again but the vast, empty plain known as the Tenere, that ran straight to the foot of the table mountain on one side and down into

Below: *A Tuareg guide.*

Left: *Roger Housden on a Sahara journey.*

Niger on the other. The tarmac only appeared seconds before we touched down, when a control tower swung into view, with three jeeps parked alongside.

The jeeps were waiting for us; one for the luggage and equipment and two to carry the ten of us. We were going to travel a couple of hours a day by jeep and then walk for the rest of the day, with breaks for meals prepared by our Tuareg guides. Except for meal times, we would spend the day in silence. We would walk alone, though in sight of at least one other person. In practice, this depended on the terrain: if we were in a canyon, then we would walk close together in snake fashion, while in the emptiness of the Tenere, we were often as much as half a mile apart. The guides would come along in the jeeps three or four hours after we had begun walking and pick us up one by one, having pointed us in a general direction at the start of the day.

The Tuareg are an ancient race who have lived in the region for millennia. They are not Arabs: they trace their ancestry to

Crete from where, it is said, they followed the salt route down into Africa. They have their own language, their own script and customs which differ considerably from their Arab neighbors. Their culture is matrilineal and it is the men, not the women, who are veiled, to keep the sand and evil spirits away from their mouths while traveling.

Our four guides were the only other people we saw during our ten days in the desert. They were surprised when they realized how we wanted to conduct our journey but happily so. They were used to Europeans passing over the landscape like voyeurs, keeping up a persistent banter and chatter quite foreign to the Tuaregs' stiller, more taciturn nature.

To walk with one of them was like walking with an antelope. Our first day or two was spent walking in a huge canyon that split open a range of red and gray cliffs which stood up straight from everywhere. Birds circled overhead and I saw the tracks of hare, snake and rabbit. On a rock lay a lizard eighteen inches long, a streak of iridescent blue. Old tree trunks

shot out shoots of new life among twisted dead branches; seed pods as large as small coconuts hung open from thorny bushes with tiny flowers as exclamatory as eyebright.

Beyond the cliffs was an empty plain, eerie and littered with black stones. In the distance loomed the stone wall of the plateau we had seen from the plane, the Tassili N'Ajjer, which means mountain of rivers. Tens of thousands of prehistoric rock paintings and engravings cover the rocks there, witness to a time some eight thousand years ago, when the land here ran with rivers, sustaining a considerable population. It was like present day African savanna; the paintings show elephants and giraffe as well as spear-carrying men, who are sometimes wearing' space-suit-like masks. We lumbered on past the Tassili. The horizon was broken only by sporadic outbursts of rock,

dropped from nowhere. Each evening after dinner, we would sit in a circle and listen for each person to voice something about their day.

After a day of walking along an old riverbed, we drove on across deepening sand through a forest of tall rock needles, to the largest dunes in the area. Nothing could have prepared us for this. The colors struck me in the chest; the desert floor was pale yellow but then the dunes were bright orange, with a sudden shift in tone here and there the higher they rose. Occasionally there would be a neatly defined band of white between the tones of orange and all of this against a sky so densely blue I felt I could plunge my arm into it. Shapes designed by the wind, each dune with its own sharp crest that wound up to a point.

With our base camp at the foot of the largest dune, each of us went out to spend twenty four hours on our own, out of sight of everyone

Right and below: *Historic rock paintings in the Tassili N'Ajjer mountains.*

Left: *The intimidating, amazing, ever-changing Sahara landscape.*

else. Some walked a mile or two over the crests, another scaled a towering rock and sat up there for the duration; one man buried himself in sand up to the neck, while others stayed close to base camp in hollows scooped out by the wind. We only used sleeping bags under the star-filled sky. Though it was fresh after nightfall, it was never cold; the days were a pleasurable 75°. I saw stars I had never seen before; I remembered the warmth that a rock can hold and the thrill of being alone in the woods as a child.

Our last days were spent walking across the Tenere. We had spent the previous night in the lee of a red cliff, the last of several we had passed on our way. When we awoke, we stared out from the shore of the cliff onto an endless sea of sand that was utterly becalmed; not a ripple, not a rock, no relief of any kind to break the mirror-like surface.

After a few hours of walking, it was obvious I was going nowhere. Where was I to go in a land that dwarfed me? When I turned back after a while to see how far I had come, the wind had already brushed my footprints away. Yet having no reference points obliged my attention to stay where I was, with this step and then that step, rather than leaping ahead to some future objective or hurdle to cross. I realized on the Tenere how our sense of self is so intricately bound up in its relation with something or someone "other," even if that other is no more than a geographical contour. Without even a contour for reference, Roger Housden himself seemed to slip away for a while, leaving little but the simple sensation of being alive–not as this identity or that, but simply as aliveness itself.

THE UPAYA FOUNDATION

THE UPAYA FOUNDATION WAS CREATED IN 1991 IN SANTA FE. It offers educational programs and retreats that encourage the practice of engaged Buddhism, a sense of ecological responsibility and solidarity and support for native peoples. With Joan Halifax as its founder, it is not surprising that wilderness retreats form a major part of the Upaya program.

Halifax's peers have called her "a woman-heart-shaman," an "authentic spirit person," an "explorer, scholar, wild woman, visionary, a true gnostic intermediary." As an anthropologist, Buddhist teacher, veteran explorer of the human mind and imaginative bridge of Buddhist and Native American traditions, she has tasted failure, reveled in success and traveled to all corners of the world. She has climbed all the mountains, lived with all the tribal peoples and made all the pilgrimages she could wish to. Now she has come home to her first love, the mountains–the foothills of the Sangre de Cristo range, on the edge of Santa Fe–where she started Upaya as a chapter of the Tiep Hien Order of Vietnamese Buddhist master, Thich Nhat Hanh.

A wilderness retreat with Joan may take the form of a pilgrimage, a prepared period of solitude, or an initiation into ceremony and ritual on the sacred land of native people. Whatever the content or the location, it will always include the rhythm of meditation practice and the underlying motive will always be the encounter with the true Self. It will not all be easy. The terrain might be arduous, the exercises might be stretching; the point is to acknowledge the Buddhist noble truth of the existence of one's own suffering and to transform that suffering, whatever its form, into compassion, for oneself and for all other beings. The rites of passage that occur on her retreats "sever you from your ordinary habitual context, move you through a threshold into a depth perspective... then return you, chastened and enriched, back into daily life." (Richard Leviton, *The Fruitful Darkness*.)

One of the retreats offered at Upaya is the Wilderness Fast, which is similar to a modern version of the Native American Vision Quest. It is primarily a practice of clarifying and seeing one's life story and of experiencing oneself on the Earth. Four days are spent in preparation,

Left & far left: *A wilderness retreat could take you to the beautiful Aguas Azules or to the Planque in the rain forest: the main focus is to experience what each landscape has to give.*

being given instruction in wilderness survival, ecological ethics, the dynamics of fasting, solitude, exposure and dreaming, and an introduction to personal myth-making and meditation. The next three days are spent in solitude, fasting in the wilderness, with the attention on the way people are and are not compassionate to themselves. Finally, the group comes together to discuss how participants can translate their inner experiences into work for the world.

The Upaya Mountain Walking Retreat takes place in the high mountains of the Sangre de Cristos in Colorado. Here, as in all her retreats, Joan encourages people to become sensitive to how deeply we are all woven into the fabric of nature; how the inner and the outer landscape can act as mirrors for each other. Meditation and mindfulness walking are the main practices for the seven days. Other retreats take people to the rain forests of Mexico and Borneo, to the Buddhist holy sites in India, to Bali and to different locations in the south-western USA. The following is a personal account by Joan Halifax of a journey into the Lacondan rain forest in Chiapas, Mexico, in 1992. It vividly conveys the atmosphere and perspectives of one of her retreats. She went with twenty-five of her friends from different cultures, including two Lacondan Indians, who acted as guides.

"In the flurry of preparation, we had little idea of what we were about to do. The day before we left, we all sat in meditation on a deck overlooking the forest and fields of Palenque. We could see patches of

Right: *The Chiapas of Mexico are less divorced from the wild forces of nature than most inhabitants of the Western world.*

old, dark green forest canopy spotted with flowers. We also saw large ravaged areas where cattle now grazed on meager fare. In the little 'forest islands' floating in the expanse of clear-cut fields, we heard small troops of howler monkeys and nearby a profusion of butterflies filled the air. At dawn, we left and made the long dusty drive through the vast deforested areas to Lacanja, a Lacondan settlement on the edge of the great forest island now protected by the Mexican government. Most of us fell into silence as we looked at the naked landscape through which we had passed. The 'three deadly Cs' have been in full force in this area for decades: cattle, chainsaws and cars. I kept remembering the Buddhist dictum, 'Nowhere to go, nothing to do.'

"As we traveled by car over rough roads through the desolation, I also remembered the Japanese expression 'mono non aware'–'the slender sadness' that arises when we remember that no matter how hard we try, life consumes life, for suffering is engendered through our very existence. Traveling to our base-camp, we go by car. This contributes to the destruction of the forest, as Pemex, the national petroleum company of Mexico, continues its invasion of the region.

"Finally, we stepped under the forest canopy. 'Going nowhere', we took many steps, each one demanding our total attention. The floor of tropical forests is a wild mass of tangled roots, the shallow soil not inviting the great old trees to penetrate but rather to spread out and seek nourishment from the earth's surface. We walked on no trails, animal trails, hunting trails and horse trails as we humbly followed our guides in their natural habitat. We were definitely not in our element. Walking required such complete attention that soon many of us fell into an absorbed if not desperate silence. The forest is a master teacher of mindful walking. One moment of wandering mind could mean a twisted

ankle, a painful fall, a close and unwanted encounter with another species. We swam in forest rivers, stood mute in wonder in clouds of butterflies, vividly scanned for snakes and signs of jaguar. And most of us never made peace with the insect population. In the end, it was the tiny and powerful presence of biting insects that brought many of us to our knees (if not our ankles). Little things mean a lot in this forest world.

"Indeed, the forest brought most if not all of us to our senses. The day after we came out, most of us felt that we had been entered by the forest as we had entered it. The forest was breathing us as we breathed the forest. As we made our way down the forest trail, the forest was making a path in us. Ten days later, as I met with friends in New York City, I realized that I was still completely embedded in my sensory system. I felt wild and over-awake, a house with all of the windows and doors wide open. Bringing the rain forest to the city in the form of milled mahogany is one thing. Bringing it into the atmosphere of the mind is something else again."

THE TRACKING PROJECT

A bushman or tracker has to know botany, astronomy, linguistics, the food chain and lots more to survive. You can get a Ph.D. in a few years but it can take all your life to become a good bushman.

John Stokes, Wingspan.

JOHN STOKES FOUNDED THE TRACKING PROJECT IN 1985 AS A non-profit organization dedicated to community education. The Project helps people gain experience of life in the natural world by teaching the traditional survival skills that Stokes first learned during six years with the Aborigines of Australia. Survival and tracking for Stokes mean not only the ability to distinguish bear tracks from wolf; they mean above all the practice of observing and listening to nature. In the process of listening, the tracker begins to develop an intimacy with his surroundings which develops into a "felt" passion and love

for the earth. In this sense, Stokes is working with the feelings, rather than just the concepts, that lead to an ecological sensibility. That sensibility extends to an awareness of the other members of the tracking party and further, to an empathy for all those peoples who still live and survive in the wild.

A significant proportion of the many thousands of people who have taken part in the Tracking Project since its inception are Native American children, who come to learn the skills that their grandfathers depended on which are in danger of being lost. Stokes and his team have run Skills Survival Camps on the Navajo Indian Reservation in Arizona and a series of expeditions in Hawaii for local children. They teach the children bush skills; making fire with fire sticks, tracking wild pig, charting their way from the stars—not just as ends in themselves but in order to encourage resourcefulness, respect, responsibility and a quality of reflection and attentiveness. Business management teams, executives of Fortune 500 companies, professionals and individuals from all walks of life come to The Tracking Project for the same reasons. Participants on a recent three-day retreat included oil industry

Left: *A father and child walk together, reinforcing their relationship with the experience.*

Previous pages: *John Stokes learned true survival skills through his work with the Aboriginal people of Australia, who continue to celebrate in their traditional cultural rôle.*

executives, environmental activists, a public radio broadcaster, three American Indian elders, a literature professor, government bureaucrats and a former member of a girl's street gang. Joseph Broz, an executive with the Houston-based Tenneco Gas Company, marveled at the fact that for three days people with such different views were able to talk to each other "without anyone going off the rails."

The Tracking Project team accomplish this by focusing not on what divides but on what people have in common, which is first and foremost the earth itself. While tracking in nature, the staff have many stories and examples to give about the interdependent relationships between man, the environment and the flora and fauna that the group meets on the way. "When you're tracking a panther in the Florida Everglades, you become more aware of how everything is linked together," commented one participant. "Very quickly, the message comes across that we're all in this together."

"When a man walks in nature," says Stokes, "his humanity is turned on and he becomes complete. That's why I sometimes describe aboriginal men as simultaneously tough and gentle. The natural world can bring this integration to full flower... People want to get some power back in their lives but we live in the world of false power. Push the button, flip the switch, turn the ignition–ooh, I'm so powerful. Power can't be grasped until you go out bush and gain the knowledge of the heart–get humbled by heat, cold, the sting of a bee, the power of a spider... Go outside and really see what is there. A friend who was trained in Guatemala tells a story of First Man, how he comes here and doesn't even know that he doesn't know. And the sun's stipulation has been that this new creation can stick around if it can survive by listening. So he listens and things begin to speak to him and he learns why he is here. The earth is telling us how to be right now if we would only listen."

As well as its community education programs, The Tracking Project provides tracking and awareness training for the general public with retreats in the south-western United States and in the Florida Everglades.

THE
SOLITARY
WAY

A LL OF THE CENTERS REFERRED TO IN THIS BOOK ARE OPEN TO individuals who want to take a personal retreat of their own design but who want to be in a meditative context that supports their need for personal silence and reflection. Most of the centers welcome individual retreatants to join in the community meditations and practices as and when it suits them; someone is usually available for discussion and guidance if needed. Pilgrims could always be sure of a night's lodging at the monastery guest house and they still can; though today you have to book, often well in advance, to be sure of a place.

I recently went on a pilgrimage to Mount Athos, a finger of land in Greece that stretches into the northern Aegean Sea. This peninsula has been the exclusive preserve of monks for almost two thousand years. Tradition has it that the Virgin Mary, along with Lazarus and Joseph of Arimathea, were shipwrecked there in a storm. Giving thanks for their lives, Mary asked God that the peninsula might be dedicated in her name and made her sacred preserve. Hermits occupied the land from the earliest centuries of the Christian era and from then on, access to the peninsula was forbidden to all women, since it belonged already to

Right: *This Buddhist hermit has spent nearly fifty years in solitude, living in a cave on a mountainside west of Peking, in order to pursue his ideal of prayer and devotion.*

Previous pages:
182/183. The immensity and solitude of the Sahara desert.

183. The monastery of Varlaam, clinging to the cliff at Meteora, Greece.

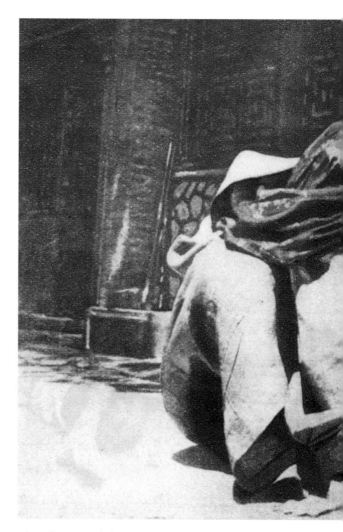

one woman alone. With the occasional exception of a female adventurer dressed as a man, no woman has set foot on the land for two thousand years. Some twenty-one monasteries of various Orthodox denominations still survive, as well as a small anchorite (hermit) population. Male pilgrims and travelers can visit the peninsula but they need a letter of introduction from their local Orthodox Archbishop. Access is by boat only, all land access being cut off by walls, fences and guards.

I went, not because I am Orthodox, or indeed particularly Christian. The idea of walking from one monastery to another through spectacular coastal scenery appealed to the solitary in me, to the romantic, to my love of beauty and wilderness and to my wish to know more of the practices of the Orthodox tradition, the most mystical of all forms of Christianity. The peninsula has no transport or roads, so the only way to travel is by foot along the paths which wind from monastery to monastery; the only places to stay are in the rudimentary guest quarters of the monasteries themselves.

I went with just one book, Ouspensky's *In Search of the Miraculous*. For two weeks I wandered those paths, talked to monks in tattered robes who practiced the Jesus prayer, saw hermits perched on cliff tops, hauling their food up from a boat in a basket on the end of a rope. I was fed by the wind and the light and barely had need of physical food; which was fortunate, since the monasteries rarely offered more than gruel and bread. Not once did I meet anyone on the path and my days were spent winding along steep slopes of loose skree, hundreds of feet above a rocky sea, in thick forests of twisted and stunted pines,

usually arriving at a monastery just before nightfall. Often, when the path was narrow, with the wind gathering around me and the sea churning far below, I would hover between fear, excitement, awe and dread. More than at any time I could remember, I felt alive. Throughout this solitary journey I felt supported by the thought that, in their own way, these monks had dedicated their lives to the same calling of the human spirit that had brought me to their land for a fortnight.

Another form of the personal retreat is seclusion, without any human support systems at all. The completely solitary retreat is another world-wide tradition that is regaining popularity today. Among tribal peoples, a young male would always mark his transition from child to adulthood by spending time alone in the wilderness. During this time, he was expected to have a vision of his life's purpose and direction. In the Anglo-Saxon tradition, the custom was to spend forty-eight hours in a tree, probably in emulation of the great deity Woden, who spent nine days and nights in a tree on his vision quest.

A vision quest is essentially a deliberate act of stopping and listening. It is to return to one's roots in nature and connect to one's own instinctual wisdom. Instead of seeking answers from outside, the attention is turned within. You find, or are led to, a sacred or powerful stretch of land; there, alone, without food, you listen and watch. Perhaps you speak to a tree or a river and listen for their response; you watch the flight of birds, or for animals and insects in the brush. You watch the rise of the stars and the planets and look for the first glimmer of day. And you feel your fear of being alone, of being unprotected; the fear of life itself, which for so many of us is hidden

behind the busyness of a normal talk-filled day.

The Vision Quest has been revived as a contemporary rite of passage. There are some organizations which offer it specifically for adolescents. One of these is Inner Adventures, in England. Some of the young people had these comments to offer on their return from the quest:

"This way of feeling, sensing and believing was very new for me. It brought me clarity and many insights into myself, nature, my life, feelings and other people. I now feel protected, ready to begin anew and am more certain who I am, what my strengths and weaknesses are, what I want to change and keep and what I wish from my life."

"The insights I got helped me to face my fears and work with them. I experienced as well an energy and trust in myself that I was not aware of... I was amazed by my "inner voices." They just had so many things to say to me and covered so many subjects. I discovered an extraordinary person to talk to and that was myself!"
(*Kindred Spirit Magazine.*)

All the major religions have their anchorite traditions where individuals choose to spend all or a portion of their life in seclusion. The hermits on Athos are continuing the practice of the early Christians who went into the Egyptian desert to pray and to face the "Tempter." Christ himself, who spent forty days in the wilderness, was the original model. It was and remains a work for the strong of heart and mind; there were many in the first few centuries after Christ who lost the good fight and ended up mad. This was so common that special monasteries were established in the Sinai desert for those individuals whose minds had become unhinged. The hermits on Athos, like those attached to the Coptic monastery of Saint Anthony in the Red Sea Desert (the first of all Christian monasteries), do not choose their lifestyle solely according to their own wishes. They start out as monks of a monastery and, after some years, if they have the aptitude and the inclination, the community assents to their spending some periods alone, outside of the monastery. When they have shown that they can successfully lead the solitary life for an extended period, they may be

Below: *Egypt: a retreatant who chooses to spend his life making supplication in the arms of a date palm.*

Left: *The building of these small Grecian monasteries in such impossible situations was an expression of extreme devotion. Now, devotees worship and pray here in solitude and deprivation.*

given permission to adopt it as a permanent lifestyle. Even then, they are still attached to a particular monastic community and visit their spiritual elders from time to time. The collected writings of the desert fathers, known as *The Philokalia*, are the heart of Orthodox Christianity's wisdom teachings. The discussion and advice to be found there on the method of the Jesus prayer–the original Christian mantra–is still followed today by contemporary practitioners on Athos.

The desert fathers had their counterparts in the mountain hermit tradition of China, which still continues today in the remote Chinling mountain range. Unlike Saint Anthony and his brothers, who were partly on the run from an unsympathetic Roman administration, the Chinese hermits were the most respected people in the world's oldest society. As the Tao te Ching indicates, rulers and kings always sought out hermits for their counsel and around 2300BCE, the Emperor Yao passed over members of

his own family and chose a hermit as his successor. The early hermits–shamans and Taoists–were later joined by Buddhists and their methods were often exchanged freely and brought into a synthesis by individual practitioners.

Why did they–and why do they still–live out a life in a cave half-way up a sheer rock face that can only be reached by a mountain climber? *The Chuangtzu*, a text some two and half thousand years old, gives us a clue.

"Let your mind be still and pure. If you want to live forever, don't exhaust your body or its vitality. Your eyes should see nothing. Let your spirit take care of your body and your body will last forever. Concentrate on the inside. Ignore the outside. Knowledge will only harm you." If you do this, it says in the *Kaoshihchuan*, the earliest book about China's hermits, "You'll stare at things like a new-born calf without looking for reasons." (Bill Porter, *Road to Heaven*.)

ASSAKREM:

A DESERT MOUNTAIN RETREAT

I N THE LAST DAYS OF NOVEMBER 1993, I WAS TRAVELING IN A battered jeep from the Algerian town of Tamanrasset to Assakrem, the highest mountain in the Hoggar range of the south-western Sahara. Assakrem, a tabletop mountain some 10,000 feet high, is the home of two Christian brothers of the Catholic Order, The Little Brothers of the Desert. They have three or four tiny retreat huts scattered around the perimeter of the tabletop and I had obtained permission to stay in one for a week.

After a long day's ride, the jeep dropped me at the foot of the mountain and I wound my way up the path that led to the Brothers' hut. They greeted me with a smile and with barely a word, led me to a hut on the far side of the tabletop perimeter. Built of the volcanic stones that lay scattered everywhere, with a corrugated iron roof, it was divided into two parts, each with its own outside door: a tiny living quarters, with a bed, a camping stove and a table; and a chapel that was bare except for a stone slab of an altar, adorned with a

picture of Christ and an animal skin on the floor. Outside, a small courtyard had been carved out of the skree and enclosed with a low stone wall. I had brought my own food and would see no-one for the week I was there.

I stood in the courtyard and gazed out on the spectacular world I had entered: phallic pillars of red rock, ridges twisted into sleeping giants, huge boulders strewn at random by the force of some ancient volcanic eruption; mountains in the shape of pyramids, saddlebacks, tabletops; valley floors of dust and sand, an old river bed snaking its way off to the east. Heavy clouds hung trails of vapor over the crests, while on the horizon the mountain waves were shrouded in dust. I stood there until dusk and watched a crack of gold slit open the gray in the west. Two birds danced along the courtyard wall, then flew off into the void. A faint flurry of pink and the day was done. The dun color of earth pervaded sky and land. I peered out over the fading view. "This is my religion," I said out loud.

Two days later, it was all rather different. I had discovered that they wear you down, the wind, the rocks, the altitude. Trying to think straight in a wind that whipped through my coat from one direction, then stopped suddenly only to start up again from another side. The door creaked even when shut and the iron roof flapped all night. Looking at rocks for hours on end: nothing else, no green, no life, no relief from the burning ground. And this at an altitude which already had my head as light as a balloon when I woke in the morning. Nothing moved there; only the sun behind the clouds. I could hear the pulse in my ears. The habitual self withers without its customary props.

For the first two days I never opened the door to the chapel; my church was outside, in the wind and the light. On the third evening, I was sitting with my eyes on a small icon of Christ Pantocrator that was on the desk of my little room. Suddenly I got up and opened the chapel door. It was dark in there and as I stooped to enter, something softened inside.

Right: *Meditation huts in Assakrem.*

When I first arrived I talked to myself aloud, then mentally. Gradually my soliloquies were replaced with silence. To begin with I was afraid of my own boredom and depression. I pushed them away with reading and writing. As the days passed the sense of boredom disappeared, even when I was doing nothing, which was most of the time. I began to sit in the chapel darkness three or four times a day. I started to sense how, even more than natural beauty, it is the awareness of one's poverty that opens the heart. To my own surprise, I began to feel some understanding, sympathy even, for the Christian teaching of original sin which has been perverted and turned into a dogma of oppression for centuries. Yet beneath all the layers of distortion lies a deep and profound teaching. My own nature–all human nature–contains a built-in fault line that severs me from authentic living. There is no blame in this; rather it is the genuine seeing of it that is required. Out there on that mountain, there was no soothing balm: even the beauty was hard-edged. The desert reduces everything to essentials, to whitened bone. There was no choice but to let go and offer my own divisions to whatever there might be–call it God, the Presence, the Self–that was more real than the contents of my own mind. I returned from that week smaller, silenced and grateful.

HALVET:

THE FORTY DAY SUFI RETREAT

---

*Take refuge in that cave; God will spread His
grace over you and will endow you—whatever
your (outward) condition—with all that your
souls may need.*

Koran

IN 1993, A BOOK WAS PUBLISHED IN GERMANY
called *40 Tage*, which describes the day to day
experience of the author in a traditional "halvet,"
or forty-day Sufi retreat. Michaela Ozelsel, born
in Germany and raised in Turkey, wrote her
book at the request of her Turkish Sufi master,
under whose guidance she completed the
solitary retreat. Ozelsel completed her
doctorate in Clinical Psychology in the USA and
this is apparent in the book, the second half of
which is a survey of research material which hopes to
explain and substantiate the experiences she underwent during
the forty days. When I asked her to describe the background to the
halvet, she wrote the following.

"The word "halvet" is etymologically derived from the
Arabic "khala," i.e. emptiness, denoting the void which
existed before the Act of Creation. Halvet is the core
exercise of the Islamic Dervish Path, the traditional
spiritual training ground of the Sufis. In an
historical sense, the practice goes back to the
Prophet Muhammed, who used to withdraw into
a cave in the mountain Hira for extended periods
of solitary meditation. Similar cross-cultural
practices can be traced back to the Palaeolithic period,
indicating that the methods used are as old as
humankind's quest for transcendental knowledge itself.

"The purpose of a halvet is not individual enlightenment, neither is
it asceticism or isolation for their own sake (Islam is extremely

Right: *A Prophet's Cave of Light: Saudi Arabia.*

Left: *Michaela Ozelsel.*

community oriented, isolation is not seen as a virtue). These are but the outer means to develop spiritually in order to better yet serve mankind. Islam states that the love for the Creator should be expressed by loving His creatures. Thus the time of withdrawal is temporarily limited, usually to forty days. Then the adept has to re-enter the everyday world, in order to actually live the higher truths that s/he may have been gifted with. The entire practice is seen as an act of worship and of sacrifice undertaken for the benefit of all humanity rather than personal gain.

"It is with full awareness that the seeker is supposed to enter the halvet, as if "going to the grave." This means leaving no unfinished business behind on any level, saying one's farewells as if seeing one's relations for the last time. This means a willingness for complete surrender to whatever will occur; a complete, trusting self-surrender to the Higher Power. In Sufic terminology, the process of spiritual development is referred to as "to die before you die," meaning the death of self-centered, egotistical parts of the human being, which keep him from realizing his Divine potential.

"After the traditional ablutions, the Sheikh–the Sufi Master–will recite the appropriate prayers and "seal" the disciple into a small chamber. Traditionally caves or cracks under large trees were used for such purposes. Nowadays, tiny, darkened, preferably bare rooms have to suffice. For forty days and nights there will be no contact with anyone, no daylight, no physical movements besides the ritualized movements involved in carrying out the obligatory prayers five times a day; neither food nor water from before sunrise till after sunset. The disciple will sleep as little as possible and spend his waking hours meditating, praying and reading selected materials such as the Holy Koran and the writings of specifically chosen Sufi saints.

"Food intake is severely restricted, just enough to keep from starving; four or six dates, occasionally a few olives or an apple, as much water as desired. The resulting weight loss can be severe. All of the foods are provided at the outset, so as to ensure that there will be absolutely no contact with anyone throughout the forty days. Although the room is locked, this is a symbolic gesture, as the disciple is also given a key. Should s/he walk out, the halvet is terminated, regardless of how valid the reasons for the disruption may have been.

"From a Western medical perspective, the entire ordeal of extreme sensory and physical deprivation is considered dangerous, physically as well as psychologically. Psychotic episodes, even death, are anticipated, as these methods have the potential to cause significant physical and mental shifts by inducing electrolyte imbalances, hypoglycemia, dehydration, sleeplessness and loss of sensory input. Achterberg's observations of Native American Vision Quests (in her book, *Imagery in Healing*) led her to conclusions which also apply to the halvet: "In short, they seem willing to push their bodies to the physiological limits in order to awaken the mind. What the modern world regards as dangerous threats to health, even to life itself, are viewed by the shaman as routes to knowledge."

Western research shows that altered states of consciousness (ASC) induced by practices as described above lead to neurophysiological states which are conducive to "the erasure of previously learned

responses, changes of beliefs, loss of memory and increased suggestibility. The ASC experiences may lead to a greater control of one's own physiology and, in breaking down the individual's habitual experience of his/her world, help overcome ego-centered problems, fixations and isolation. The transcendental and unitive experiences associated with these ASC reflect the individual going beyond dualistic perceptions of self and conscious ego/unconscious self separation, thereby achieving psycho-spiritual integration and growth." (M Winkelmann, *Yearbook of Cross-Cultural Medicine and Psychotherapy*.)

"To the disciple undergoing this archaic, yet transtemporal sacred practice, it is not the scientific understanding that matters. It is the transformation s/he experiences in his/her entire being, in the heart,

Left: *Sufi master watching over his disciple and retreatant.*

Far left: *Kela M'Guna Sufis in Morocco, preparing to embark on retreat.*

body, mind and soul. It is the gift of visions and visionary dreams, the encounters with long-deceased saints of the tradition, it is the awe and wonder of the transcendental realms, of which glimpses might be granted and which cannot be discussed within the confines of human language and ordinary consciousness. It is the resulting 'certainty of knowledge', which goes far beyond mere speculation to the very Essence of Being.

"And finally it is the responsibility which goes along with the privilege of having received permission to undergo this ancient sacred ordeal; to actually live this knowledge which has been granted, beyond the halvet, out there in the everyday world. The extent to which this is happening might be the final criterion for differentiating an actual transformation-in-progress from self-delusion and imagination."

Ozelsel's own retreat took place in Istanbul, in a tiny room where she could hear the sound of the television in the next flat, the beating of carpets and the shouts of children outside in the street. She had electricity (when power cuts permitted) and a bathroom. In the evening of the last day, the Sheikh came and recited prayers outside her door for peace in the world and that her prayers should be accepted. When she finally met him and he asked how she was, she found that she hardly had any voice. "Don't bother talking," the Sheikh told her. "Listen. Listen to the world around you." The following is a rough translation of her diary entry on the fortieth day.

"The Holy Koran speaks about Light above light but here, grace above grace is visible, gratitude above gratitude fills me. Now tears of joy arise in me. How grateful I am for everything. Grateful for gratitude... forty days. What wisdom lies precisely in this span of time. Not more, not less... so grateful. I feel immersed in gentleness, acceptance, trust, inner peace. I ask for protection for "outside" in order to "remember" when the real tests come. I ask that the veil of forgetfulness should never close again, that my attitude of arrogance and self-importance should be surmounted by this love and mercy. How much has been given me. May I have the strength to pass it on wherever I can, like 'a bridge over troubled waters.' "

Michaela Ozelsel's Sufi Master is Dr. Oruc Guvenc. Guvenc is a Clinical Psychologist and Music Therapist at the University of Istanbul, as well as being a Sufi Master in various Dervish traditions, including the Mevlevi, the Rufai and the Bektashi. He visits Europe regularly and runs groups in Germany, Austria and Spain.

THE TIBETAN
THREE YEAR RETREAT

*I said good-bye to my wife... Then we
proceeded in formal procession behind Rinpoche,
our retreat director and other lamas to the gates
of the men's retreat. The sealing ceremonies
were done outside in a cold rain, where liturgies
were read by a car's headlights... we entered the
retreat one by one and the door closed.
We would not see the outside world
for three years and three months.*

Ken McLeod, Buddhist America.

Below & right: *Retreatants on a Tibetan Kagyul retreat.*

Previous pages: *196/197. Participants in a three-year Tibetan retreat at the Kagyul Retreat Center, France.*

197. The Temple at Kagyul Retreat Center, France.

THE THREE YEAR RETREAT IS PART OF THE KAGYU TRADITION OF Tibetan Buddhism. It is a systematic training in advanced meditation techniques which takes place in a totally isolated location. A group of practitioners take the retreat together, under the direction of a lama, though the only contact with fellow retreatants is during the group ceremonies and rituals. The individual eats his meals in his cell and practices meditation there sixteen hours a day. Various Kagyu centers now offer an opportunity for this retreat in America, Scotland and France. Recent attendance figures suggest its growing popularity among Western Buddhists: in 1993, ninety people were enclosed in the Three Year Retreat beginning at the Kagyu center in the Dordogne, in France, while at the same time, thirty-five more ended their retreat on Holy Island, in Scotland. It offers a unique context in which practitioners can give their entire attention and commitment to the intricate and subtle work with the mind that Tibetan meditation practices demand.

Retreatants prepare themselves theoretically beforehand, with teachings on Buddhist texts, lessons in Tibetan and in the playing of the ritual instruments. They will each pay approximately $5000 US for the retreat. A typical retreat day will begin at 4.00AM with a two-hour meditation and end at 9.00PM. Several times a month there will be major rituals in the temple instead of the normal individual meditation sessions. While the schedule remains approximately the same throughout the retreat, the actual meditation practice will change and pass through the key Kagyu techniques.

What is clear to most practitioners at the end of their retreat is how short a time three years is for the study and practice of such a deep inquiry into the mind as Tibetan Buddhism makes available. Far from expecting the retreat to end with enlightenment and freedom from suffering, most people who have completed the three years see it as a firm foundation on which to build their ongoing practice in everyday life. The real retreat, as one retreatant emphasized to me, is after all the retreat of one's own mind in the midst of everyday activity.

Below: *To make the ultimate retreat is to retreat from the everyday, into one's center.*

Right: *Retreats can take place in a moment, by simply observing a sunset or a flower.*

THE ULTIMATE RETREAT

THE REAL RETREAT IS, AFTER ALL, THE RETREAT OF ONE'S OWN MIND IN THE MIDST OF EVERYDAY LIFE.

To be able to live fully in life without being tossed this way and that by every passing mood and whim; to know a place of silence in oneself that subsists even when all around is chaos and confusion, to maintain equanimity in the face of doubt and despair: this, perhaps, is the ultimate retreat of one's own mind, the aspiration of spiritual practitioners of every Way and tradition.

When you take a formal retreat within a spiritual tradition, you are laying the foundations for this inner retreat. Such equanimity may seem a long way from your present reality–it is for most of us–but if you just start now by taking a retreat of any kind–one that feels most in accord with your needs and your nature–you will be giving yourself a precious gift.

You are giving time to yourself: time to feel your own feelings, think your own thoughts and sense your own individuality and priorities. You are permitting a return to yourself, and in that return you will begin to see yourself and your life with fresh eyes. For that return is a foretaste of the inner place of retreat which in truth is never far away–after all, it is none other than who you are.

THE FOLLOWING IS A LIST OF ADDRESSES AND WHERE POSSIBLE, telephone numbers, for all the retreat centers discussed in this book. Those discussed in this book are marked with a star ( ). The list is categorized by discipline, according to the chapter headings, with additional sections at the end for holistic and new age retreat centers.

THE WAY OF KNOWLEDGE

BUDDHISM

Amaravati Buddhist Monastery, St. Margaret's, Great Gaddesden, Hemel Hempstead, Hertfordshire, UK, HP1 3BZ.

Dharma Dena, HC-l, Box 250, Joshua Tree, California, USA, 92252. Tel: 619 362 4815.

○ Gaia House, Woodland Road, Denbury, Near Newton Abbot, Devon, UK, TQ12 6DY. Tel: 0803 813188.

○ Insight Meditation Society, 1230 Pleasant Street, Barre, Massachusetts, USA, 01005. Tel: 508 355 4378.

○ Insight Meditation West, PO Box 909, Woodacre, California, USA, 94973. Tel: 415 456 8940.

International Meditation Center, PO Box 13314, Suite 111, Oakland, California, USA, 92252. Tel: 301 461 8946.

London Buddhist Vihara, 5 Heathfield Gardens, London, UK, W4 4JU. Tel: 081 995 9493.

ZEN BUDDHISM

○ Ch'an Meditation Center, 90-31 Corona Avenue, Elmhurst, New York, New York, USA, 11373.

Empty Gate Zen Center, 1800 Arch Street, Berkeley, California, USA, 94709. Tel: 415 548 7649.

○ Plum Village, Meyrac, Loubes-Bernac, 47120 Duras, France. TEL: 010 33 53 947540.

San Francisco Zen Center, 300 Page Street, San Francisco, California, USA, 94102. Tel: 415 863 3136.

Shasta Abbey, PO Box 199, 3612 Summit Drive, Mount Shasta, California, USA, 96067. Tel: 916 926 4208.

○ Sonoma Mountain Zen Center, 6367 Sonoma Mount Road, Santa Rosa, California, USA, 95404. Tel: 707 545 8105.

Throssel Hole Priory, Carrshield, Hexham, Northumberland, UK, NE47 8AL. Tel: 0434 345204.

Western Zen and Ch'an Retreats: Winterhead Hill Farm, Shipham, Winscombe, Avon, UK, BS25 1RS.

Zen Center of Los Angeles, 923 South Normandie Avenue, Los Angeles, California, USA, 90006. Tel: 213 255 5345.

TIBETAN BUDDHISM

✪ Dzogchen Beara, Garranes, Allihies, West Cork, Ireland. Tel: 027 73032.

✪ Holy Island Retreat Center, and Samye Ling Tibetan Center, Eskdalemuir, Langholm, Dumfriesshire, Scotland, UK, DG13 0QL. Tel: 03873 73232, Fax: 03873 73223.

✪ Lerab Ling, L'Engayresque, 34650 Roqueredonde, France. Tel: 010 33 6744 4199.

✪ Rigpa International Center, 330 Caledonian Road, London, UK, N1 1BB. Tel: 071 700 0185.

Rigpa USA, PO Box 607, Santa Cruz, California, USA, 95061-0607. Tel: 408 454 9103.

The Nyingma Institute of Colorado, 1441 Broadway, Boulder, Colorado, USA, 80302. Tel: 303 443 5550.

The Nyingma Institute, 1815 Highland Place, Berkeley, California, USA, 94709. Tel: 415 843 6812.

RAJA YOGA

Himalayan International Institute, R. R. L, Box 400, Honesdale, Pennsylvania, USA, 18431. Tel. 717 253 5551.

✪ The Self-Realization Fellowship UK: Tel 071 286 1524.

✪ The Self-Realization Fellowship, 3880 San Rafael Avenue, Los Angeles, California, USA, 90065-3298. Tel: 213 225 2471, Fax: 213 225 5088.

✪ The Brahma Kumaris World Spiritual University, 401 Baker Street, San Francisco, California, USA, 94117. Tel: 415 563 4459.

✪ The Brahma Kumaris World Spiritual University, Global Harmony House, 46 South Middle Neck Road, Great Neck, New York, New York, USA, 11021. Tel: 516 773 0971.

✪ The Brahma Kumaris World Spiritual University, The Global Retreat Center, Nuneham Park, Nuneham Courtenay, Oxford, UK, OX44 9PG. Tel: 0867 38551, Fax: 0867 38576.

SHAMANISM

Bear Tribe Medicine Society, PO Box 9167, Spokane, Washington, USA, 99209. Tel: 509 258 7755.

✪ Kahuna Retreats, Aloha International, PO Box 599, Kapaa, Hawaii, USA, 96746. Tel/Fax: 808 822 9272.

✪ The Sundance Ceremony, C/O Carol Youngson-White Owl, 47b Westbourne Road, Sheffield, UK, S10 2QT. Tel: 0742 682762.

✪ The Sundance Ceremony, The Deer Tribe Metis Medicine Society, 11259 East Via Linda Street, 100-142 Scottsdale, Arizona, USA, 85259. Tel: 602 443.3851.

✪ The Sweatlodge Ceremony, C/O Leo Rutherford, Eagle's Wing Center for Contemporary Shamanism, 58 Westbere Road, London, UK, NW2 3RU. Tel: 071 435 8174.

THE WAY OF THE HEART

CHRISTIANITY

The Abbey Community [Interfaith], The Abbey, Sutton Courtenay, Near Abingdon. Oxfordshire, UK, OX14 4AF. Tel: 0235 847401.

The Center for Creation Spirituality, St. James' Church, 197 Piccadilly, London, UK, W1V 0LL. TEL: 071 287 2741.

The Christian Meditation Center, 10 Grosvenor Road, Glen Iris, Victoria, Australia, 3146. Tel: 03 822 4870.

The Christian Meditation Center, 1130 Westchester Place, Los Angeles, California, USA, 90019. Tel: 209 897 3711.

The Christian Meditation Center, 29 Campden Hill Road, London, UK, W8 7DX. Tel: 071 937 0014.

The Christian Meditation Center, 4b 322 East 49th Street, New York, New York, USA, 10128. Tel: 212 831 5710.

Friends of Creation Spirituality, C/O ICCS, Holy Names College, Oakland, California, USA, 94619. Tel: 510 436 1206.

New Camaldoli Hermitage [Roman Catholic], Big Sur, California, USA, 93920. Tel: 408 667 2456.

✪ Osage Monastery, 1870 West Monastery Road, Sand Springs, Oklahoma, USA, 74063. Tel: 918 245 2734.

Omega Order [Interfaith], The Priory, Winford Manor, Winford, Bristol, UK, BS18 8DW. Tel: 0275 872262.

Our Lady of Guadaloupe Trappist Abbey [Interfaith], PO Box 97, Lafayette, Oregon, USA, 97127. Tel: 503 852 0107.

✪ Shantivanam Retreats, Saccidananda Ashram, Shantivanam, Tannirpalli (PO) Kulithalai, Trichy (DT), Tamil Nadu, India, 639107. Tel: 91 4323 3060

✪ The Taize Community, F-71250 Taize, Cluny, France. Tel: 85 50 1414.

SUFISM

The Sufi Healing Order, 38 Russell Terrace, Leamington Spa, Warwickshire, UK, CV31 1HE. Tel: 0926 422388.

The Sufi Order International, 23 Rue De La Tuillerie, 92150 Suresnes, France. Tel: 010 33 47 284846.

✪ The Sufi Order of the West, PO Box 30065, Seattle, Washington, USA, 98103. Tel: 206 782 2001.

BHAKTI YOGA

✪ Amritanandamayi Ashram, M A Math, Kuzithura PO (Via Athinand), Quilon District, Kerala, India.

Amritanandamayi Center, PO Box 613, San Ramon, California, USA, 94583. Tel: 415 537 9427.

Amritanandamayi, Maison Amrita, BP88, 68160 Ste Marie Aux Mines, France. Tel: 89 58 59 56.

✪ Ram Dass Retreats, C/O The Hanuman Foundation, 105 Sunnyside Avenue, San Anselmo, California, USA, 94960. Tel: 415 457 8570.

✪ Ram Dass Retreats, C/O The Open Gate, 1 Woodman's Cottage, Brockham End, Bath, UK, BA1 9BZ. Tel: 0225 428557.

THE WAY OF THE BODY

TAI CHI

- ✿ Al Huang Retreats, C/O The Living Tao Foundation, PO Box 846, Urbana, Illinois, USA, 61801. Tel: 217 337 6113.

  Living Tao Siftung, Postfach 3531, CH4002 Basel, Switzerland. Tel: 61 361 5375.

  Living Tao UK. C/O Julia Lavelle, 127 Lee Park, Blackheath, London, UK, SE3 9HE.

- ✿ The School of Tai Chi Chuan, 5th. Floor, 47 West 13th Street, New York, New York, USA, 10011. Tel: 212 929 1981.

YOGA

- ✿ Kripalu Center, Box 793, Lenox, Massachusetts, USA, 01240. Tel: 413 448 3400.

  Kripalu Retreats, Amrit House, 24 Tregew Road, Flushing, Falmouth, Cornwall, UK, TR11 5TF. Tel: 0326 377529.

  Mount Madonna Center, 445 Summit Road, Watsonville, California, USA, 95076. Tel: 408 847 0406.

- ✿ Yasodhara Ashram, Box 9, Kootenay Bay, British Columbia, Canada, V0B 1X0. Tel: 604 227 9224.

SUPRAPTO MOVEMENT WORK

Helen Poyner, 6/11a Emmerick Street, Leichhardt 2040, New South Wales, Australia.

- ✿ Suprapto Suryodarmo, Mojosongo Seminar, PO Box 301, Solo, Jawa Tengah, Indonesia.

THE WAY OF ART

- ✿ Caroline Mackenzie, C/O Cosmic Images Retreat, Sandeepani, 5 Danyrallt, Llaneglwys, Builth Wells, Powys, UK, LD2 3BJ. Tel: 0982 560 315.

  Frederick Franck, C/O Zen Of Seeing Retreats, Hazlewood House, Loddiswell, Near Kingsbridge, South Devon, UK, TQ7 4EB. Tel: 0548 821232.

- ✿ Frederick Franck, C/O Zen Of Seeing Retreats, C/O Pacem In Terris, Covered Bridge Road, Warwick, New York, New York, USA, 10090.

THE WAY OF SOUND

- Chloë Goodchild, Naked Voice Retreats, C/O 1 Woodman's Cottage, Brockham End, Bath, UK, BA1 9BZ. Tel: 0225 462450.

- Jill Purce, 20 Willow Road, London, UK, NW3 1TJ. Tel: 081 444 4855/071 794 9841.

THE WAY OF THE WILDERNESS

- Sahara Walk, The Open Gate, 1 Woodman's Cottage, Brockham End, Bath, UK, BA1 4BZ. Tel: 0225 428557.

- The Tracking Project, Box 266, Corrales, New Mexico, USA, 87048. Tel: 505 898 6967.

- Upaya Foundation, 1404 Cerro Gordo Road, Santa Fe, New Mexico, USE, 87501. Tel: 505 986 8518.

THE SOLITARY WAY

HALVET: THE FORTY DAY SUFI RETREAT

✪ The Academy for Traditional Central Asian and Turkish Music, Jahngasse 38, A-1050 Vienna, Austria. Tel/Fax. 0222 545 7920.

THREE YEAR RETREAT PROGRAMS

Chakpori Ling Foundation [Nyingma lineage], 10400 Highway 116, Forestville, California, USA, 95432. Tel: 707 887 7859.

Dhagpo Kagyu Ling, Landrevie, 24290 Montignac, Dordogne, France.

Samye Ling Tibetan Center, Eskdalemuir, Langholm, Dumfriesshire, Scotland, UK, DG13 0QL. Tel: 03873 73232.

HOLISTIC AND NEW AGE CENTRES

These centers offer a very wide variety of workshops and retreats covering many of the categories in this book.

Breitenbush Hot Springs Retreat Center, PO Box 578, Detroit, Oregon, USA, 97342. Tel: 503 8S4 3314.

Esalen Institute, Big Sur, California, USA, 93920. Tel: 408 667 3000.

Findhorn Foundation, The Park, Forres, UK, IV36 0RD. Tel: 0309 673655.

Harbin Hot Springs, PO Box 782, Middletown, California, USA, 95461. Tel: 707 987 2477.

Lama Foundation, PO Box 240, San Cristobal, New Mexico, USA, 87564. Tel: 505 586 1269.

Omega Institute, 260 Lake Drive, Rhinebeck, New York, USA, 12572. Tel: 914 266 4444.

Achterberg, J. *Imagery in Healing: Shamanism in Modern Medicine*. Boston: Shambala, 1985.

Aelred, Dom. *Contemplative Christianity–An Approach to the Realities of Religion*. New York: Seabury Press, 1974.

Anon. *The Cloud of Unknowing*. London: Penguin Classics, 1961, 1983.

Batchelor, Stephen. *The Faith to Doubt*. Berkeley: Parallex Press, 1990.

Berendt, Joachim Ernst. *Nada Brahma*. London: East-West Publications, 1988.

Berry, Wendell. *The Landscape of Harmony*. Hereford, Herefordshire: Five Seasons Press, 1987.

Bloom, Archbishop Anthony. *Living Prayer*. London: Darton, Longman & Todd Ltd., 1966.

Bodian, Stephen and G. Feurstein, editors. *Living Yoga*. New York: Jeremy Tarcher, 1993.

Brown, Tom. *The Journey*. New York: Berkeley, 1992.

——. *The Quest*. New York: Berkeley, l991.

——. *The Vision*. New York: Berkeley, 1988.

Carretto, Carlos. *Letters From the Desert*. London: Dartman, Longman & Todd Ltd., 1972.

Castaneda, Carlos. *The Teachings of Don Juan: A Yaqui Way of Knowledge*. London: Penguin Books Ltd., 1967, 1990.

Crook, John. and David Fontana, editors. *Space in Mind*. Shaftesbury, Dorset: Element, 1990.

Crook, John. *Catching a Feather on a Fan*. Shaftesbury, Dorset: Element, 1991.

Deshpande, P. D. *The Authentic Yoga*. London: Rider, 1978.

Doore, Gary, editor. *Shaman's Path*. Boston: Shambala, 1988.

Fox, Mathew. *Original Blessing*. Santa Fe, N. M: Bear & Co., 1983.

Franck, Frederick. *The Awakened Eye*. New York: Random House UK Ltd., 1979.

——. *The Zen of Seeing*. New York: Wildwood House, 1978.

Gerard, Geoffrey. *Away From It All: A Guide to Retreat Houses and Centers for Spiritual Renewal* [Christian retreats only]. Cambridge, UK: The Lutterworth Press, 1989.

Godman, David, editor. *Be As You Are: The Teachings of Ramana Maharshi*. London: Penguin Books Ltd., 1992.

Goodchild, Chloë. *The Naked Voice*. London: Rider, 1993.

Hanh, Thich Nhat. *The Miracle of Mindfulness*. Boston: Beacon, 1987.

Kadloubovsky, E. and G. E. H. Palmer, translators. *Writings from The Philokalia on the Prayer of the Heart*. London: Faber & Faber Ltd., 1951, 1992.

Kandy, Nanamoli. *The Life of the Buddha*. London: Mandala, 1978.

Kelly, M. and J. Kelly. *Sanctuaries: The West Coast and South West: A Guide to Lodgings in Monasteries, Abbeys, and Retreats in the USA*. New York: Bell Tower Publications, 1993

——. *Sanctuaries: The North-East*. New York: Bell Tower Publications, 1991.

Lane, John. *Art and the Sacred*. Hartland, Devon: Green Books, 1988.

Man-Ho Kwok, M. Palmer, J. Ramsay, translators. *Tao Te Ching*. Shaftesbury, Dorset: Element Books, 1993.

Merton, Thomas. *Contemplative Prayer*. London: Darton, Longman & Todd Ltd., 1973.

——. *Seven Storey Mountain*. London: SPCK. 1990.

——. *Zen and The Birds of Appetite*. New York: New Directions, 1968.

Morreale, Don, editor. *Buddhist America: Centers, Retreats, and Practices*. Santa Fe, New Mexico: J. Muir Publications, 1988.

Needleman, Jacob. *Lost Christianity*. San Francisco: Harper SanFrancisco, 1980.

Novak, Philip. *Parabola Magazine*. New York: Summer Issue 1990.

Ozelsel, Michaela. *40 Tage*. Munich: Diederichs, 1993.

Porter, Bill. *Road to Heaven*. San Francisco: Mercury House, 1993.

Purce, Jill. *The Mystic Spiral: Journey of the Soul*. London: Thames and Hudson Ltd., 1974.

Radha, Swami. *Hatha Yoga–The Hidden Language*. Spokane, Washington: Timeless Books, 1987.

Rinpoche, Sogyal. *The Tibetan Book of Living and Dying*. San Francisco: Harper SanFrancisco, 1992.

Rumi, Jalal'ud-din: E. Whinfield, translator. *The Mathnawi: the Spiritual Couplets*. London: Octagon Press Ltd., 1973.

Shearer, A, translator. *The Upanishads*. New York: Harper and Row, 1978.

Sheng Yen, Master. *Getting the Buddha Mind*. New York: Dharma Drum, 1992.

Timira, Father Alphonse. *Christian Meditation Newsletter*. London: Christian Meditation Center, 1993.

Tworkov, Helen. *Zen in America*. Berkeley: North Point Press, 1989.

Whittaker, Stafford. *The Good Retreat Guide: UK, Ireland and France*. London: Rider, 1991.

Yogananda, Paramahansa. *Autobiography of a Yogi*. London: Rider, 1987.

Magazines

A Retreatant's Companion. Los Angeles, USA: The Self-Realization Fellowship, 1982.

An Introduction to Self-Realization. Los Angeles, USA: The Self-Realization Fellowship, 1982.

D'Angelo, James. *Resonances of the Cosmos*. Leamington Spa, Warwickshire: Caduceus Magazine, issue 23, 1993.

Harner, Michael. *Newsletter*. Norwalk, Connecticut: The Foundation for Shamanic Studies, summer 1986.

Hay, John. *The Immortal Wilderness*. New York: Parabola Magazine, summer 1990.

Kindred Spirit Magazine. Totnes, Devon: Kindred Spirit, 1993.

Letter from Taize [published in nine languages every two months]. Cluny, France: Taize Community.

Leviton, Richard. *The Fruitful Darkness*. Escondido, California: Yoga Journal, spring 1994.

Margaret Olmsted, *Tai Chi Press*. New York: Tai Chi Press, 1-IV, 1989.

Reznikoff, Professor Iegor. *The Therapy of Pure Sound*. Leamington Spa, Warwickshire: Caduceus Magazine, issue 23, 1993.

Samye Ling Magazine. Eskdalemuir, Scotland: Samye Ling, summer 1993.

Stokes, John. Wingspan: *Journal of the Male Spirit*. Manchester, Massachussetts: Wingspan publishing, summer 1990.

The Vision [UK journal of the National Retreat Association–Christian retreats only]. Liddon House, 24 South Audley Street, London, UK, W1Y 5DL. Tel: 071 493 3534.

Winkelmann, M. *Yearbook of Cross-Cultural Medicine and Psychotherapy*. Berlin: VWB, 1990.

—A—

altered states of consciousness (ASC), 194

America, 38, 40, 47, 48, 51, 53, 60, 64, 65, 85, 88, 109, 158, 197, 198

ashram, 99, 100, 101, 113, 132, 133, 146

Assakrem—see Desert

—B—

Bali, 175

Bhakti Yoga 2, 106, 108

Bodhidharma, 8

Brahma Kumaris World Spiritual University, 62-63, 204

Buddhism , 8, 23, 26, 29-35, 38, 44, 50, 53, 56, 57, 81, 82, 151, 174, 198

    Mahayana, 53, 58, 82

    Nyingma, **50-51**, 54, 204, 209

    Theravada, **32-33**

    Tibetan, 26, **48-58**, 198

        Gelug, 50, **53**

        Kagyu, **50**, 58, 198, 209

        Vajrayana, 53

    Zen, 8, **37-47**, 81

        Rinzai, **37-38**, 47, 53, 89

        Soto, **37-38**, 47, 53, 89

—C—

Carretto, Carlos, 82, 89, 210

Castaneda, Carlos, 64, 65, 210

Ch'an, 26, 42, 44, 203

chakra, 128, 152

Chandra Swami, 4

chanting, 2, 46, 61, 68, 72, 74, 103, 108, 111, 113, 133, 149, **151-161**, 163

    Gregorian, 152, 156

    Mongolian overtone, 158, 160

children, 46, 56, 105, 113, 179, 195

China, 8, 37, 38, 122, 124, 140, 187

Chogyam Trungpa, 51, 56, 111

Christian Meditation Centers, 94

Christian mysticism—see Mysticism

Christianity 2, 15, 22, 23, 29, 57, **79-101**, 106, 108, 116, 139, 147, 184, 187, 210

compassion, 2, 33, 58, 82, 96, 174

contemplation, 4, 21, 22, 23, 62, 79, 80, 81, 82, 87, 88, 89, 94, 95, 99

Creation Spirituality, 92, 93, 206

creativity, 92, 128, 139, 140, 145, 151, 156

Crook, Dr. John, 43, **44**, 210

—D—

Dakshinamurti, 7

Dalai Lama, 27, 53, 56

dance, 2, 22, 65, 68, 76, 98, 103, 104, 122, 125, 134, 136, 161, 165

Desai, Amrit, 130

desert, 2, 7, 19, 68, 84, 87, 169, 190

    Assakrem, **188-191**

    Sahara, 82, 98, **170-173**, 188, 208

devotion, 2, 27, 53, 60, 100, 106, 111, 112, 128, 145, 152

dhikr, 103

Dzogchen Beara, 56, 204

—E—

ecology, 57, 66, 92, 174, 175, 179

enlightenment, 17, 37, 38, 42, 96, 103, 124, 193, 198

Eros, 92

—F—

Foucauld, de, Charles, 84

Four Noble Truths, 30

Fox, Mathew, 92, 210

France, 14, 45, 51, 56, 97, 113, 156, 198, 203, 204, 206, 209

Franck, Frederick, 141, **142-144**, 207, 210

—G—

Gaia House **35**, 203

Gelug—see Buddhism, Tibetan

gnosis, 87

Goodchild, Chloë, **162-166**, 208

Greece, 85, 183

Gregorian chant—see Chanting

guided meditation—see Meditation

guru, **25-27**, 51, 53, 61, 62, **106-108**, 109, 111, 132

—H—

halvet, **192-195**

hara, 120, 121

Hindu, 18, 21, 24, 25, 100, 106, 111, 113, 119, 137, 145, 146, 148, 149, 152, 154, 163

Holy Island Retreat Center, **56-58**, 204

—I—

Ikkyu, 13

India, 4, 6, 7, 8, 30, 62, 80, 91, 96, 99, 100, 105, 106, 109, 112, 113, 130, 132, 145, 147, 148, 154, 162, 175, 206

Insight Meditation Society **34**, 203

Ireland, 56, 159, 204

Islam, 14, 102, 104, 193

—J—

Japan, 37, 38, 140

Java, 134, 135, 137

—K—

Kagyu—see Buddhism, Tibetan

Kahuna Retreats **74-76**, 205

Karma yoga—see Yoga

Kenya, 162

koan, 37, 43, 44, 91

Korea, 38, 41

Kriya yoga—see Yoga

Kripalu Center for Yoga and Health, **130-131**, 207

kundalini (see also Yoga), 127, 128, 133

—L—

lama, 53, 198

Lerab Ling **56**, 204

lodge, 70, 71, 72, 132

LSD, 109

—M—

Mackenzie, Caroline, **145-149**, 207

Mahayana—see Buddhism

mantra, 53, 88, 94, 95, 133, 152, 154, 155, 161, 187

Mata Amritanandamayi Ashram **112-113**

meditation, 17, 18, 20, 21, 34, 42, 58, 80, 88, 93, 94, 116, 130, 131, 175, 203, 206

    guided, 133, 148

metta, 33

metanoia, 90

metta—see meditation

— M (cont) —

Missionaries of Charity, 95

Monastery, 32, 87, 203, 206

Mongolian overtone chanting—see Chanting

Muhammed, 192

music, 2, 8, 98, 105, 108, 140, 152, 160, 162, 163

mystical experience, 22, 79, 81, 94

mysticism, 50, 81, 85, 88

    Christian, 88

—N—

National Retreat Association, 79

Native American, 2, 67, 70, 152, 161, 174, 179, 194

Noble Eightfold Path, 30, 31

Nyingma—see Buddhism, Tibetan and the *Nyingma Institute*

Nyingma Institute, 54, 204

—O—

Om, 149, 154

Osage, **101**, 206

—P—

painting, 46, 140, 148

Palaeolithic, 193

Patanjali, 59, 127, 131

Plum Village, **45-46**, 203

poetry, 104, 140

Pope, 81, 97

power animals, 65, 72

pranayama, 59, 127, 128, 129, 131, 132

Protestantism, 81

Purce, Jill, **158-161**, 208

—Q—

Quietism, 81

—R—

Radha, Swami **132**, 132, 133

Ram Dass Retreats **109-111**, 206

relaxation, 136, 165

Renaissance, 81, 139, 140, 141

Retreats International, 79

Rigpa, **54-55**, 56, 204

ritual, 55, 65, 66, 70, 92, 115, 147, 174, 198

Roman Church, 81

Rumi, 102, 104

Russia, 113

—S—

Sahara—see Desert

samadhi, 59

samatha, 32

Samye Ling, 56, 57, 204, 209

Sankara, 24

satsang, 24

sattipathana, 32

Scotland, 51, 56, 58, 198, 204, 209

Second Vatican Council, 81, 142

Shaikh, 103

shamanism **64-78**, 115, 205, 210

Shantivanam **99-100**, 206

Siberia, 64, 156

singing, 22, 113, 115, 140, 151, 159, 160, 162, 164, 165

Sogyal Rinpoche, 50, 51, 54, 55, 56, 197

Sonoma Mountain Zen Center, **47**

—S (cont) —

sound healing, 156

Sri Lanka, 32

Sufism, **102-105**

Sufi Order of the West, 104, **105**, 206

Sundance Ceremony, **67-68**

Suprapto, **134-137**, 207

surrender, 20, 26, 27, 91, 103, 104, 106, 108, 130, 131, 193

Suzuki, 38, 47

Sweatlodge Ceremony, **70-72**

—T—

Tai Chi, 115, 119, 120, **122-126**, 136, 207

Tai Chi Chuan—School of, **126**, 207

Taize Community, **97-98**, 206

Tanzania, 95

tension, 116, 120, 136

Theravadin—see Buddhism

Thich Nhat Hanh, **45-46**

Thomas Merton, 4, 7, 19, 38, 79, 81

Tibet, 48, 50, 51, 53, 54, 56, 155

Tibetan Buddhism—see Buddhism

Tracking Project, **178-181**, 208

Trappist, 79, 80, 206

Tree of Life, 148

Tsongkhapa, 53

Tuareg, 171

—U—

Upaya Foundation **174-177**, 208

—V—

Vajrayana—see Buddhism, Tibetan

vegetarian, 34

Vietnam, 14, 38, 45, 46

vipassana, 32, 33, 34, 35

vision quest, 185

Vivekenanda, 6

—W—

Wales, 44, 148, 207

walking, 34, 35, 41, 42, 98, 130, 136, 169, 170, 171, 172, 173, 175, 176, 184

—Y—

Yasodhara Ashram Yoga Retreat and Study Center, **132-133**, 207

Yoga, 42, 50, 53, 59, 60, 113, 119, 120, **127-137**

    Bhakti, 2, **106-114**

    Hatha, 127, 129, 130, 132, 133

    Karma, 60

    Kriya, 61

    Kundalini, 127, 130, 132, 133

    Raja **59-63**, 2, 20, 106, 127

Yogananda Paramahansa, 60, 61

—Z—

Zen—see also Buddhism, Zen, 8, 13, 14, 15, 26, 35, 37, 38, 41, 42, 44, 45, 47, 48, 53, 81, 84, 89, 96, 140, 142, 203, 207, 210

The publishers would like to thank the following people and organizations for permission to quote from their work in this book. Whilst every effort has been made to trace all present copyright holders of this material, whether companies or individuals, any unintentional omission is hereby apologized for in advance. We would be pleased to correct any errors in acknowledgments in any future editions of this book.

Batchelor, Stephen. *The Faith to Doubt*. Berkeley: Parallex Press, 1990.

Berendt, Joachim Ernst. *Nada Brahma*. London: East-West Publications, 1988.

Berry, Wendell. *The Landscape of Harmony*. Hereford, Herefordshire: Five Seasons Press, 1987.

Bloom, Archbishop Anthony. *Living Prayer*. London: Darton, Longman & Todd Ltd., 1966; Springfield: Templegate Publications, 1966.

Bodian, Stephen and G. Feurstein, editors. *Living Yoga*. New York: Jeremy Tarcher, 1993.

Crook, John. *Catching a Feather on a Fan*. Shaftesbury, Dorset: Element, 1991.

Franck, Frederick. *The Awakened Eye*. New York: Random House UK Ltd., 1979.

Harner, Michael. *Newsletter*. Norwalk, Connecticut: The Foundation for Shamanic Studies, summer 1986.

Kadloubovsky, E. and G. E. H. Palmer, translators. *Writings from The Philokalia on the Prayer of the Heart*. London: Faber & Faber Ltd., 1951, 1992.

Lane, John. *Art and the Sacred*. Hartland, Devon: Green Books, 1988.

Merton, Thomas. *Contemplative Prayer*. London: Darton, Longman & Todd Ltd., 1973; originally published as *The Climate of Monastic Prayer*. Kalamazoo: Cistercian Publications, 1969.

Morreale, Don, editor. *Buddhist America: Centers, Retreats, and Practices*. Santa Fe, New Mexico: J. Muir Publications, 1988.

Needleman, Jacob. *Lost Christianity*. San Francisco: Harper SanFrancisco, 1980.

Olmsted, Margaret. *Tai Chi Press*. New York: Tai Chi Press, 1-IV, 1989.

Porter, Bill. *Road to Heaven*. San Francisco: Mercury House, 1993.

Sheng-yen, Master. *Getting the Buddha Mind*. New York: Dharma Drum, 1992.

An Introduction to Self-Realization. Los Angeles, USA: The Self-Realization Fellowship, 1982.

Kindred Spirit Magazine. Totnes, Devon: Kindred Spirit, 1993.

A Retreatant's Companion. Los Angeles, USA: The Self-Realization Fellowship, 1982.

The extracts on pages 38 and 47 are reprinted with permission from *Zen in America: Five Teachers and the Search for an American Buddhism*, by Helen Tworkov. Published in 1994 by Kodansha America Inc., New York. Copyright 1989 by Helen Tworkov. All Rights Reserved.

Abbey of St. Hildegard: 92, 93. Ahmuno: 5, 29, 40, 48 top, 50, 54, 55, 56 bottom left & right, 57, 59, 201.

Amrit Trust: 131. Bodleian Library: 104. Bernard Boulanger: 23, 24, 154, 196-199.

Brahma Kumaris World Spiritual University: 62, 63. John Crook: 25, 42-44 (both).

Gianluca De Santis: 26, 53 right, 67, 180. Mary Evans Picture Library: 85.

Format Partners Picture Library: 124, 125, 163. Frederick Franck: 140, 142, 144. Friends of Amma: 112, 113.

Gaia House: 35 (both). Gamma Presse: {Christian Vioujard: 20, 79, 88; Arkell/Spooner: 33; Laurent Maous: 39;

Alexandre Figour: 48 bottom}; 69, {Alexis Georgeon: 80, 89; Francois Lochon: 90; Jean Marc Loubat: 178;

Peter Robinson/Liaison: 179}. Glasgow Herald: 58. Michael Holland: 137. Arne Hodalic: 13.

Roger Housden: 4, 78, 83, 84, 86, 99, 100 (all), 162, 164, {Chloe Goodchild: 170}; 171, 172, 174-177, 182, 188-191, 200.

Images Colour Library Ltd: 37, {Horizon: 49}; 60, 65, 74, 75, 122, 123, 153, 183. Image Select: 53 left, 151, 184.

Insight Meditation Society: 34 (both), 41. Bruno Kortenhorst: 128. Kripalu Center: 115, 117, 118, 127, 130.

Hanuman Das: 109, 110 (both), 111. Caroline MacKenzie: 145, 146, 148, 149. J. Minihan: 161.

Farida Montgomery: 138. National Palace Museum, Taiwan: 8. Osage Monastery: 94, 101 (all).

Osho Foundation: 18, 106, 107, 120. Dr. Michaela Ozelsel: 192. Edna Palian: 16, 135, 143, 150, 169.

Klaus Paysan: 64, 168. Plum Village: 36, 45 (both), 46. Premgit: 129, 166, 218.

Qiu Zeng Ping/photographer Gary Woods: 15. Leo Rutherford, Eagle's Wing: 70 {Liddy Papageorgiou: 71 all}, 72, 73.

Samye Ling Tibetan Centre: 56 top right. Peter Sanders Photography: 7, 9, 21 bottom, 27, 102, 103, 187, 193-195.

Self-Realization Fellowship: 61. Mike Shoring: 28. Sonoma Mountain Zen Center: {Reinhard Gorner: 30; Dale McCarty: 47}.

Taize Community: 97, 98. John Walmsley: 158, 159. Yasadhara Ashram: 132, 133.

Zefa Pictures: 1, 2, 3, 6, 10, 14, {Bob Croxford: 21 top}; 32, {Hermann Schlenker: 52}; 66, 68, 77, 81, {Starfoto: 91}, 114,

{J. Hackenberg: 141}; 157, {A. Jones: 173 left; Sunak: 173 right; Heinz Steenmans: 186}.

Picture Research: Image Select International/Dora Goldberg.

Every effort has been made to trace all present copyright holders of the material used in this book, whether companies or individuals.
Any omission is unintentional and we will be pleased to correct any errors in future editions of this book.